THE ALTON BUS CRASH

THE ALTON BUS CRASH

JUAN P. CARMONA

Published by The History Press
Charleston, SC
www.historypress.com

Copyright © 2019 by Juan Carmona
All rights reserved

Cover image courtesy of the *Monitor*, April 19, 1993, 2D.

Facing page, top: NTSB diagram of the accident. *Courtesy of the National Transportation Board Accident Report HAR-90-02.*

Facing page, bottom: NTSB map of the Rio Grande Valley and the location of the accident site. *Courtesy of the National Transportation Board Accident Report HAR-90-02.*

First published 2019

Manufactured in the United States

ISBN 9781467143615

Library of Congress Control Number: 2019940046

Notice: The information in this book is true and complete to the best of our knowledge. It is offered without guarantee on the part of the author or The History Press. The author and The History Press disclaim all liability in connection with the use of this book.

All rights reserved. No part of this book may be reproduced or transmitted in any form whatsoever without prior written permission from the publisher except in the case of brief quotations embodied in critical articles and reviews.

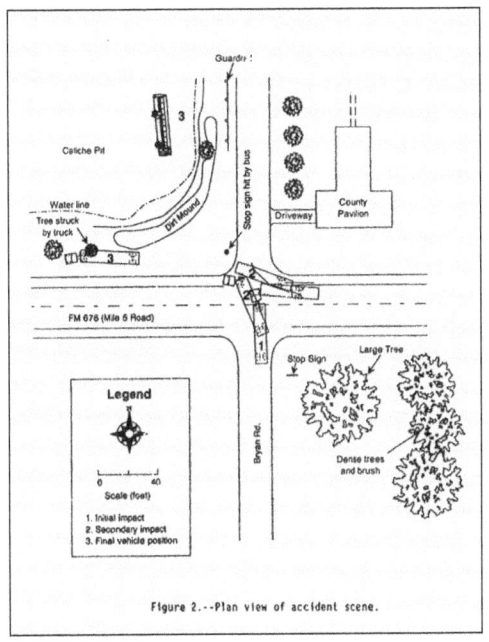

Figure 2.--Plan view of accident scene.

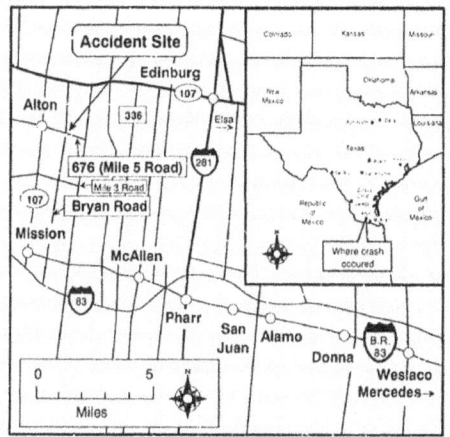

Figure 1.--Map of accident location.

Dedicated to the twenty-one young lives that ended on September 21, 1989, as well as the survivors, the families, the community and everyone else who was touched by the events of that day.

Picture of the caliche pit today. *Courtesy of Jack Bloodworth.*

CONTENTS

Acknowledgements	11
Prologue: Walking Home from School	13
Introduction	15

PART I: THE ACCIDENT
The Men	23
Collision	26
Outside the Bus	39
Community	47
School	52
A Darkness Descends	57
The Investigation	60

PART II: THE COURTS
The Criminal Trial of Ruben Perez: The Prosecution	67
The Criminal Trial of Ruben Perez: The Defense	73
The Lawsuits	78
Alex's Story	81
LULAC	82
Barratry and Lawsuits	89

PART III: AFTERMATH
Survivors and Community	93
Changes	99

Contents

Conclusion	103
Notes	107
Bibliography	115
Index	123
About the Author	127

ACKNOWLEDGEMENTS

This book in its technical form is a culmination of years of research and interviews, a project that began years ago when my brother and I had a small production company and I posed the idea of producing a documentary on the subject. This was before the emergence of social media, and the internet was not as pervasive a tool as it is today. We were only able to contact a few people, and the project never came to fruition. However, about two years ago, I was approached by Andy Zavala (my cousin's husband) to assist him with a documentary on the subject. I cannot thank him enough for facilitating my reentry into the subject. He used his resources to obtain many of the interviews, which assisted me with the completion of this project, and I look forward to continuing to assist him with his film project and see that come to fruition as well. Additionally, I would like to acknowledge the help I obtained from Ms. Maria Oralia Barrera with the editing of the manuscript and Ms. Alondra Chapa, who helped me organize my research, both of which made the writing of this book much easier. Finally, I would like to thank Mr. Ben Gibson of The History Press for taking an interest in getting this story told.

On the other hand, when it comes to acknowledging the people who helped bring about the completion of this book, there are no words that can express the gratitude I have to those who sat down to share their stories with me. These were difficult conversations to have, whether it was in person or over the phone, but they shared their stories nonetheless. I will be forever grateful. This story has touched so many people, and the positive results from such a tragic incident will no doubt continue to save lives into the future.

PROLOGUE
WALKING HOME FROM SCHOOL

It was the usual hot Valley afternoon, and my cousin Gabriel and I were walking home from school. We could feel the heat radiating from the black asphalt as we walked alongside old Highway 83. The highway ran the length of the Rio Grande Valley where I grew up. As the valley developed, it and the railroad tracks that are parallel to it were usually the dividing point between rich and poor, Anglo and Mexican. In Donna, where I grew up, it was the southern side for the Mexicans and the northern side for the Anglos. One could easily assess this as you drove north and south of the city. For other cities in the Valley, it was the opposite; however, there was always some sort of division.

As we walked along the highway toward my house, we could feel the hot wind of the cars that flew by us and kicked up some of the ever-present dust, which accumulated on all things during periods of drought. We had just come up to a neighborhood corner store that was along the way when a bus passed us, and just as it did, the emergency door flew open and a young Mexican boy was flung out of the bus and landed on the road just before us. I froze. I can still see him lying there on his stomach a few feet away from me, his head turned to the left. I heard a *crack* as he hit the ground. His mouth was slightly open, and either from his mouth or his head, there was bright red blood running along the black asphalt. I stood frozen and stared, shocked, fascinated and afraid because I did not know what to do. The bus kept going, unaware it was minus one passenger.

Prologue

This was a time before cellphones or even 911, a time when you actually had to memorize numbers, and at that moment my mind was blank. My cousin, on the other hand, knew exactly what to do. We ran toward the store and were met by the clerk, who had seen what had happened from behind the counter. My cousin yelled, "Call the police!" The clerk looked just as befuddled as myself: "I don't know...." "464-4481," Gabriel yelled at him. "Call 464-4481!" The young man from the store stood frozen, looking beyond us to the poor boy bleeding his life away on the asphalt. Gabriel ran in and made the call.

I wish I could write more about what happened that day, but that is all I can recall. I didn't even go home and tell my family. I just went home, listened to the news and heard that he was leaning against the emergency exit lever when it opened. That story has stayed in the recesses of my mind since it happened. Every time I hear about a school bus accident, the image of that boy lying on the ground, with the color of the blood against the asphalt, is what pops into my mind. That was the first image that came to me on September 21, 1989, when someone came into Mrs. Morales's Spanish class and said that there had been a bus accident and some students had been killed.

It was my first brush with death, and sadly, for those students aboard Mission school bus no. 6, it was theirs as well. Except their experience was deeply personal, for although I did not know the boy who died on the road before my eyes, these students were intimately connected to the victims. They were their brothers, sisters, cousins, friends and schoolmates. Their losses would leave a profound mark on them, their families and their community. For them, the words *tragedy* and *loss* are not strong enough; indeed, there is no combination of words, nor a book, nor volumes of books, that could ever truly define their loss.

INTRODUCTION

ALTON, TEXAS

The city of Alton, Texas, is located in the South Texas border region known as the Lower Rio Grande Valley. Most residents of the area refer to it as the RGV (Rio Grande Valley), or simply the Valley. The city was founded during a time of great change in the Rio Grande Valley. Its economy was shifting from a ranching to agricultural economy through the introduction of irrigation and railroads. In fact, it is from a railroad that the city gets its name, the Alton Railroad Company from the city of Alton, Illinois. The town was established in 1911 with an initial population of fifty residents.[1]

Railroads came to the RGV through a concerted effort of men like Richard King, John Kenedy, Jim Wells, John Armstrong and Robert Driscoll, all of whom had within prior decades acquired large tracts of land from Mexican American landowners who were forced to sell due to a drop in cattle prices, drought and inability to pay taxes, as well as through less than honorable methods (this was a period of violence and terror for the Mexican American community of the Rio Grande Valley). These men saw the acquisition of this land as an investment whose return would come from a change in economies from ranching to farming. However, in order to sell the Valley as a place to make money in agriculture, the area needed to be connected to the national market, and that meant a railroad was needed. However, Southern Pacific refused on the grounds that it would not be a profitable investment. So, these men funded the creation of a railroad in the Lower Rio Grande Valley.[2]

Introduction

Alton Water Tower. *Photo by author.*

The combination of the connecting of rails to the Valley and the creation of irrigation districts succeeded in bringing about this transition.

Despite the fact that the Valley's main industry was switching to agriculture, this was not the industry on which Alton would be centered. Alton's product would be the very ground on which it was founded. The city would provide caliche (sedimentary rock) for construction products throughout the country.[3] Tragically, caliche extraction and the pits it created would be indelibly linked to the heartbreak that occurred on September 21, 1989.

The city grew slowly. It maintained its own post office from 1913 to 1916, after which it was run out by the larger neighboring city of Mission. It would be the same story for its school. This schoolhouse was your typical rural six-grade school, named Alton School after the city. It was first managed under the Hidalgo County school superintendent, but like the post office, it was annexed into the Mission Consolidated Independent School District (CISD). This school still exists as Alton Elementary within the Mission School District—it was a Mission school bus that the students were riding on that calamitous day.[4]

Alton would not be officially chartered until April 1, 1978. In its infancy, the city manager, mayor and four aldermen met in a rented room. Eventually, they were able to purchase a church house, which became city hall. In time and through federal housing grants, the city expanded its services, providing all the major utilities to its residents. Then it began to promote more commercial development, and the city slowly began to grow. At its birth in 1978, Alton elected its first mayor, Ms. San Juanita Zamora. She was the mayor of the city during the Alton school bus tragedy.[5]

Life for the students who boarded Mission CISD school bus no. 6 was pretty much a shared experience, in that they were all around the same age and attended the same schools (high and middle school). The caliche pit was the biggest "attraction" in their neighborhood, for it was a place all the students were very familiar with and played around. Many of them played hide-and-seek or simply hung out around the very pit the bus would fall into. There was no barrier or fence to keep them away from the area (one of the many issues whose solutions would be demanded after the accident). Another hangout spot for the kids in the neighborhood was the pool at nearby Palm Lake Estates apartment complex. In an interview, a survivor pointed out, "It was kind of sad because we would all swim and most of these people drowned, and you don't expect that. I didn't expect it, and it hurts now, really hurts."[6]

The neighborhood itself, at that time, attracted very little commercial development. There were no big chain grocery stores like H-E-B or Walmart. It was mostly small neighborhood stores where families would shop for the essentials, or where kids would walk over for candy or a cold drink on hot Valley days. In the neighborhood lived a man named Roque Sosa, who had a small ranch with horses and chickens. He offered the children jobs feeding the chickens and horses and grooming them. He let the children ride the horses, and at times, he gave some of the boys money for helping to break the horses. His home was another local fixture where neighborhood kids could be found.[7]

1989

The year 1989 would prove to be one of the most tragic and sensational years in the history of the Rio Grande Valley. In July of the previous year, another catastrophe occurred in the Rio Grande Valley in the border in the city of Brownsville. On July 7, the city experienced a heavy downpour of rain that happened over a very brief period of time. The water accumulated on the roof of La Tienda Amigo (a retail store), causing the roof and the rest of the three-story building to collapse on the occupants, which included workers, shoppers and people who were simply trying to get out of the rain. The accident resulted in fourteen deaths and forty-seven people injured. The incident made national headlines as people watched the rescue effort unfold. Rescuers included local, state, federal authorities and even international help (people who had worked in the recovery effort after the Mexico City Earthquake of 1985 offered their expertise to the rescue effort), much like what would occur with the Alton Bus Crash. People held their breath, waiting

Introduction

to see if anymore survivors would be pulled out of the debris.[8] Exponent, an engineering and scientific consulting firm, made some conclusions about the cause of the tragedy:

> *The Amigo Store building was constructed without benefit of engineering. Structural steel beams and columns were stacked in "building-block" fashion without regard to structural stability. The ad hoc design was barely strong enough to carry the added weight of the third story and stored inventory. A few inches of water dumped on the roof by the intense downpour was all it took to trigger instability and the resulting catastrophic collapse.*[9]

The nature of the collapse led to a series of lawsuits, which played themselves out at the same time as those that made their way through the courts from the Alton Bus Crash. The suits came to an end in 1990 with a settlement of $33 million.[10] These suits, along with the ones from the school bus accident, painted the Rio Grande Valley as a place that was "friendly" to lawsuits. Due to this perception that the RGV was an area that "paid out," two national cases, against Goodyear Tires and Vioxx, were both tried in the Valley. Nonetheless, given the lawsuits and the sad events in Brownsville, that tragedy was on everyone's minds during 1989.

One of the most infamous stories to come out of 1989 was that of the death of Spring Breaker Mark Kilroy. South Padre Island was and still is a very popular destination for Spring Breakers and vacationers to the Rio Grande Valley. It is located off the coast of Port Isabel, which is a short drive from Brownsville, where you can cross the bridge into the Mexican border city of Matamoros. Matamoros is actually older than its sister city of Brownsville and was always the hub of international commerce and intrigue. Brownsville lay at the outskirts of Matamoros until the Mexican-American War firmly placed the border as the Rio Grande River, and thus Brownsville was created due to it being cut off from Matamoros by the new international boundary. Fort Brown was established to protect the frontier; however, citizens of both cities maintain amicable relations to this day.

The attraction for Mark Kilroy and his fellow Spring Breakers was essentially that Mexico was so close to the island and its drinking age, eighteen. Underage drinkers could drink their fill in Matamoros. (Crossing into Matamoros for a good time has become less prevalent with the advent of the drug wars and the violence that erupts from time to time in these Mexican border cities.) There was so much money to be made during Spring Break that bars and clubs in Matamoros opened only once a year during

Introduction

the month of March. This was the draw for Mark Kilroy and thousands of others who crossed the International Bridge into Matamoros; sadly, for Mark, he would not return from one of these trips.

It was a typical humid early Tuesday morning as Mark Kilroy and his friends Bradley Moore, Bill Huddleston and Brent Martin walked toward the International Bridge to cross from Matamoros back to Brownsville. They walked among the mass of other Spring Breakers also headed back to the United States. Along the way, Mark stopped to talk to a girl he had recently met. His friends slowly walked ahead to wait for him, and then Bill ran behind a tree to urinate. He then rejoined the others, who were waiting at Garcia's Bar for Mark, who never came. He had been snatched by Serafin Hernandez, a member of a drug dealing family whose power had been growing ever since they had become associated with Adolfo de Jesus Constanzo, a practitioner of Palo Mayombe. The religion used parts of human bodies, obtained through grave robbing, for some of its ceremonies; however, Adolfo hypothesized that one could gain even more power through live human sacrifices, so he began to demand humans for sacrifice from the Hernandezes, promising increased wealth and protection from harm. Indeed, some of the members revealed to the press after the fact that they thought themselves bulletproof.[11]

The demand for humans to sacrifice may have seen extreme to some, but the Hernandez family had expanded their power through ruthlessness. In fact, during their rise to power, there were dissenting voices from other family members, who then disowned the Serafin Hernandez faction. Sadly, one member of the family was killed, cut to pieces, placed in a backpack and left at the grandmother's residence by the river.[12] So, Constanzo's request was agreed to, and soon they began taking members of rival cartels and whomever crossed their paths. They all disappeared along with others who were caught up in the shift of drug trade routes through South Texas. Unfortunately for Mark Kilroy, Adolfo believed that he would gain more power from his rituals if he were to sacrifice an Anglo.

So, that early Tuesday morning, Serafin Hernandez sat in a truck and searched through the Spring Breakers who walked passed him for a victim. He was not alone. There was another group of gang members in another truck who would be the ones to snatch Mark off the streets of Matamoros. He ended up at the Hernandez ranch outside the city, where Adolfo arrived and lead the ceremony, during which Mark was sacrificed and decapitated.[13] The disappearance, the search and the murder made international news. The gruesome details fed into the perception of the "uncivilized" border with dark, shadowy areas into which one could disappear. In truth, this story was shocking to people on both sides of the border, and it would be a story that continued to be told to youngsters who planned on going to the island or Mexico for Spring Break.

Needless to say, the year 1989 would be a traumatic one for residents of the Rio Grande Valley. It would scar those who lived through it and painted the Valley in a certain light to outsiders, most of whom would go on to see the Valley as an outlier and a place where juries paid out large sums of money. However, of all these incidents, the one that would have the biggest and most lasting impact, not only on the lives of those directly touched by the tragedy but also for every family who placed their children on a school bus, would be the event that occurred on September 21, 1989.

HOPE, BUSES AND TRAGEDY

Every year, either late in August or in the beginning of September, sleepy-eyed children and parents make their way to a bus stop. Parents sometimes stand with their children and wait until the bus comes or appoint an older child to watch over their younger siblings. On the other hand, the parents may feel that they are old enough to wait for the school bus on their own. Each of these children/students carry with them the hopes and dreams of the previous generation. In migrant communities, success at school meant a better life for their children, and this was the driving factor behind why they are in this country. As a result, students sometimes carry the weight of the struggle their parents undertook for them to come to America, and this steers them toward success in their schools.

Point in fact, compulsory school attendance harkens back to the 1800s, when labor unions were vying for workers' rights, better pay, safer working conditions and the end of child labor, which was tied to free education for their children. Many workers saw themselves stuck in an endless cycle of labor until they could not work anymore. Indeed, for them, there was no real avenue for advancement, and therefore, there would be no improvement to their living standards. As a parent, sacrifice is part and parcel to what one endures in raising children. Consequently, although unions pushed for better pay and working conditions, they knew that those goals would make life a little more comfortable, but there would be no great social mobility for them. The type of advancement they wanted for their children required

Introduction

education, so that is one of the main goals they worked toward. This was also why they pushed for an end to child labor. If children were legally obliged to be in school, then they would not (for the most case) be employable.[14] As a result, the working class and those in poverty sent their children to America's schools year after year, so that they could make a better tomorrow for themselves.

In a way, one could look at the school bus as a symbol of hope. For even though public school is free, this does not mean that every young child in America has the ability to get from his or her home to school. Furthermore, unlike free lunch, there are no requirements to ride the bus other than residing along the bus's route. Therefore, even if a family did not have a car or parents had to work, the bus was there for them, a tool to facilitate their educational success. Here it came, down the road lit by the morning sun or streetlights or sometimes no lights at all except for its headlights, picking up the most prized possession parents can possess: their child. The future of America is currently rolling down the nation's roads, picking up and dropping off students from school and even, at times, taking children to football games, academic competitions and field trips to museums or local areas of interest. Sometimes a bus would take kids out of town and to places where, without the school, some students would never have been able to go, providing them with invaluable experiences that will help their character grow. Big, noisy and yellow—hope is found in a bus.

This is what makes this story so tragic and, at times, triumphant. Instead of a bus being seen as a symbol of hope to Americans everywhere, it was the symbol of unspeakable tragedy. In the Rio Grande Valley, the loss of twenty-one innocent lives will always be linked to a school bus. One cannot disconnect the memory of one from the other. The images are permanently connected—the hopes and dreams of not just the parents but the children whose potential never came to fruition and whose goals would never be accomplished.

PART I
THE ACCIDENT

THE MEN

September 21, 1989, was a crisp, cool morning—the type of morning Valley residents enjoy because temperatures like eighty degrees are rare even in September. The border region known as the Rio Grande Valley of South Texas is situated in a subtropical climate, and the weather consists of what seems like an eternal summer of high heat and high humidity, with some cooler days in the spring and short bursts of cold winds during the winter. Consequently, eighty degrees for people in the Valley was time for a light sweater, or for some a thicker one (depending on the child and the parent). However, one thing that eighty degrees in the Rio Grande Valley meant was that on a school bus, most of the windows would be shut. In 1989, most school buses did not have air conditioning or heat, so the windows were the only way to attempt to regulate the temperature inside the vehicle. Students who felt cold and found their window to be open could reach over and pull them up. Closing a window on a school bus required engaging the latches on both ends of the window at the same time. This would release the window and allow you to slide it up. This maneuver would prove to be very difficult for the students involved in the accident.

The morning of the accident, forty-six-year-old bus driver Gilberto Pena woke up at his usual 5:30 a.m. According to the National Transportation Safety Board (NTSB) report, Mr. Pena had a Class A driving license with no

The Alton Bus Crash

The Monitor newspaper's front page from the day of the accident. *From* The Monitor, *September 21, 1989.*

restrictions, which allowed him to drive all types of large vehicles, including a school bus. Also in the report was the fact that he had a relatively safe driving record, with a speeding ticket and one minor traffic citation for a failure to yield. However, on September 21, he would be on the receiving end of someone else who failed to yield, with deadly consequences. Pena was prescribed glasses but never wore them and was not wearing them the day of the accident. He stated to the investigators that the reports stating the need for glasses "were an error."[15]

September 21 began as a normal day for Gilberto; he got up and took a shower to wake himself up and get going for the day. As he showered, his wife prepared him some breakfast so that he could eat before he started his long day. Mr. Pena did not live far from the bus barn, and when he finished his breakfast, his wife drove him the four blocks to the Mission Consolidated Independent School District's bus depot. He arrived at the bus barn at 6:45 a.m. Once there, he followed his usual duties, which included a pre-trip inspection of the bus to ensure that it was safe to take out on the road. This was the same bus he had been assigned that year, and he was quite familiar with it. He then took time to give the bus a cleaning, picking up whatever may have been left behind or the errant wrapper or paper that kids tucked into the seats or threw into a corner. With his daily maintenance duties done, he prepared to head out on his route.[16]

His route took him on two morning and two afternoon trips, due to the size of the district and the number of buses. A bus driver's trips consisted of his or her first run to pick up the elementary students and the second run to pick up the middle and high school students. This is why different grade level schools have different start and end times, to maximize and facilitate the picking up and dropping off of students.

The driver of the Dr Pepper truck owned by Valley Coca-Cola Distributors was twenty-six-year-old Ruben Perez. Mr. Perez's driving record stands in stark contrast to that of Mr. Pena. Much like Mr. Pena, Ruben possessed a Class A driver's license that was also unrestricted. His driving record reveals that he had a speeding ticket in 1984, and on February 5, 1987, he was cited for property damage while driving a truck for Valley Coca-Cola. According to the report, he was on a divided highway that was wet from some recent rains, and he "failed to control his speed," causing him to strike another vehicle. His failure to control his speed would play a part in his collision with the school bus as well. He would go on to be cited again for speeding and twice for not having liability insurance on his automobile.[17]

His employment history with Valley Coca-Cola has him beginning as a loader in August 1984. Every distribution truck has two employees, the driver and the loader who assists the driver in unloading the beverages and delivering to the various businesses on their route. Perez eventually was promoted to driver, but after the accident in February 1987, he was demoted back to loader. There he remained until he was eligible to return to driving on May 11, 1989. His promotion was delayed due to his license being suspended for the failure to have liability insurance citation along with a failure to appear citation, an issue he promptly corrected and was allowed back on as a driver. One additional note in the NTSB report is that he had no real formal driver's training. His father was a truck driver, and he went on to teach his son his trade.[18]

COLLISION

Gilberto Pena was on his second run to pick up students from the small town of Alton who attended school at the nearby Mission Consolidated Independent School District. His first trip consisted of sleepy-eyed kindergarteners who were still adjusting to leaving their parents and their homes to head to a strange new place, filled with other children their age and a new parental figure in the teacher. They were accompanied by other older elementary students who were still adjusting to their new school year. These young students met at a pickup point located one block shy of Bryan Road and Business Highway 83. He boarded the children and took them to Bryan Elementary. The trip went by uneventfully, and he left the elementary school to his second pickup route, which consisted of the older kids, middle and high school students. This route would take the bus along Farm to Market Road 676 and Bryan Road.[19]

The area where the students were being picked up was a rural spot with unpaved streets. In fact, the streets were "paved" using the caliche, which the early residents of Alton had quarried as one of the earliest industries in the city. The morning routine for many of the students was to meet outside one another's houses and then walk the quarter mile to the nearby paved road where the bus would stop to pick them up.[20] This was due to the fact that the bus could not navigate well through the dirt roads and in times of rain might even get itself stuck in the mud or be unable to see the large potholes that riddled the streets.

The Accident

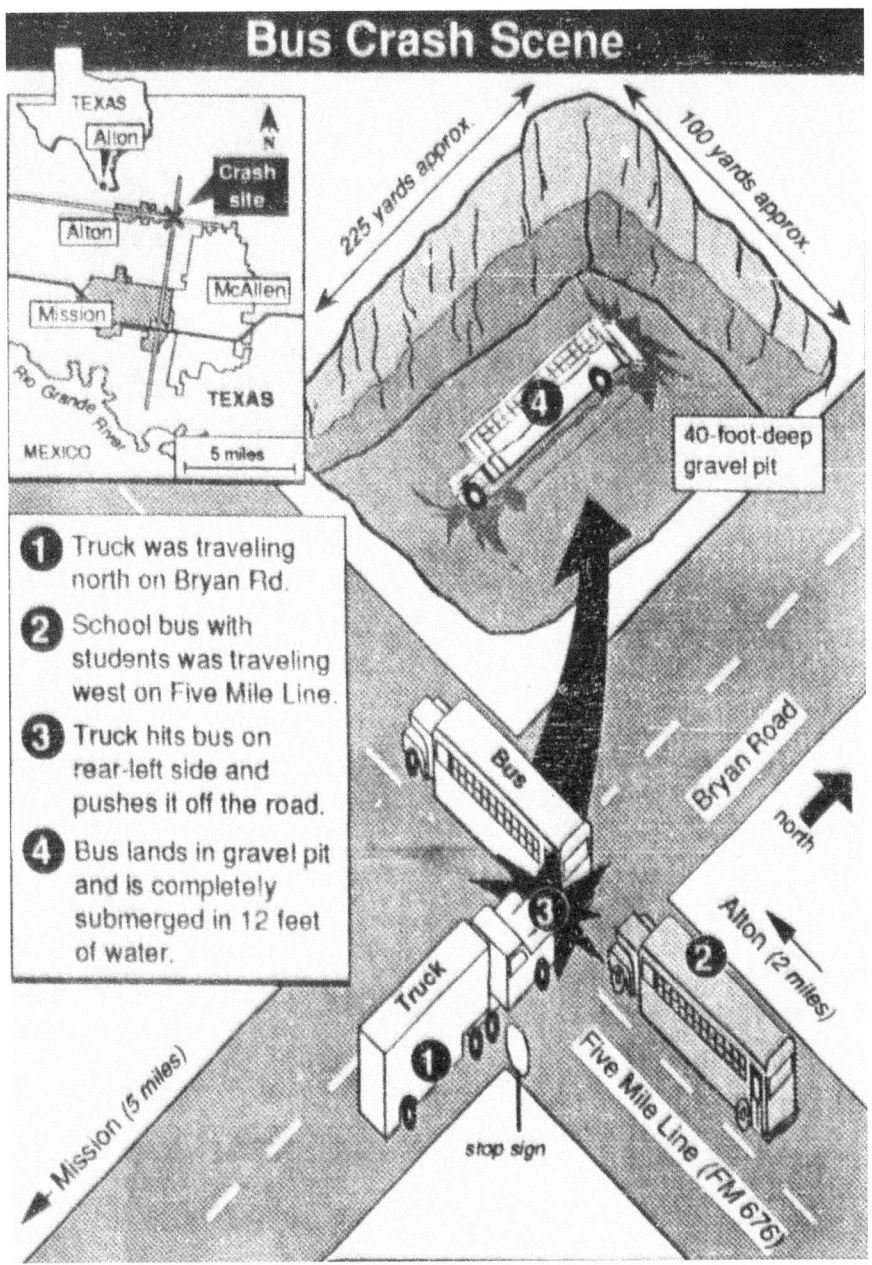

Texas Department of Public Safety diagram of the accident. *From* The Monitor, *September 22, 1989.*

Early morning temperatures caused the students to have most of the twenty-eight- by thirty-one-inch windows closed; survivors stated that only two or three were open.[21] The bus was filled with the chatter, laughter, giggling and banter of its young occupants. The sunny sky above reflected the sunny dispositions of the students; although they might not have been happy about going to school, for the moment they were with their peers, siblings, cousins, friends and neighbors. Any time and any day these youths got to spend with their friends outside of having to learn was a good time. For some, this was the whole reason to go to school, to spend time with their friends, make new friends, joke around, find love and live the classic American dream with football games, homecoming, prom and graduation.

At 7:34 a.m., Mission Consolidated school bus no. 6 picked up the last two passengers, bringing the total number of occupants to eighty-one students.[22] Meanwhile, the Dr Pepper truck driver, Ruben Perez, and his loader, Ruben Pena (no relation to bus driver), completed their first stop for Valley Coca-Cola at the Circle K convenience store. The clerk reported that they left at about 7:20 a.m. These students were just beginning their lives, and for far too many, their lives would end that day. Truly, the lives of everyone on board that bright yellow bus—and for those who survived, those who had never been exposed to death or tragedy of any kind—would never be the same. Additionally, those who participated in this event—rescuers, nurses, witnesses, law enforcement and members of the media who covered the incident—would all see their old lives end. What would be left was a new life that would be forever shaped by that day and the compounded tragedy that ensued from it.

Perez's Dr Pepper truck left the convenience store and then continued north on Bryan Road toward Alton.[23] At the same time, the atmosphere in Mission bus no. 6, as described by survivor Virginia Flores, was normal, with groups of kids "chit-chatting" with their friends, passing the time as they made their way to another school day.[24] Those who were lucky enough to find a seat were sitting with their friends, while others were standing. The bus itself was very crowded. Eighty-one occupants placed it just under the eighty-three-passenger limit for which the bus was designed. The bus was manufactured by the Blue Bird Bus Company and was part of the "All American" series of buses. Each side of the bus had fourteen rows of seats designed for three passengers, with the seat directly behind the driver smaller, affording space for two.

It is important to point out that at the time of the accident, the school bus was built to code and was in compliance with the specifications and

The Accident

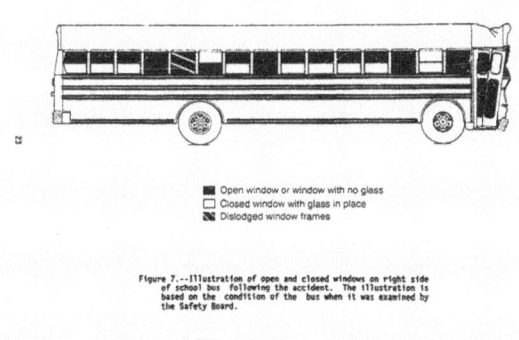

NTSB illustration of which windows were opened and which were closed on the bus at the time of the accident. *Courtesy of the National Transportation Board Accident Report HAR-90-02.*

regulations of the time. As a result, the events that unfolded could have happened with any other school bus in Texas, and from this tragedy some good would come regarding the manufacturing of safer buses.

Although the bus's specifications dictated that all students should have a seat, there were kids standing at the time of the accident, whether it was to visit with their friends or because they did not want to sit on the seat that was directly over the tires because there was a large hump on the floor of the seat. Also, like school buses today, there were no safety belts for the passengers, only the driver. Exiting the bus was accomplished through the front side door, and in case of emergencies, the emergency door in the rear of the bus opened through the use of a lever that would be lifted up. For most of the victims of the accident, there were the aforementioned twenty-eight- by thirty-one-inch windows.[25]

Today, the area where the crash happened, the corner of Bryan Road and FM 676, contains a stoplight and a fenced enclosure around the caliche pit into which the bus fell. The pit was large, with a width of 385 feet, a length of 610 feet and a maximum depth of 40 feet. On the day of the accident, the pit was filled with about 10 feet of water, just enough to cover the bus as it came to rest on its side. On September 21, 1989, there was no fence surrounding this huge pit. It was completely open to the road. It was an accident waiting to happen, and sadly, one had already occurred in a nearby pit that was open to the road as well.[26]

On May 28, 1989, two Alton teenage boys crashed their car into this other open caliche pit, leaving a sixteen-year-old passenger dead. Their car swerved into the pit and flipped, landing on its top; both of the passengers were ejected from the vehicle. The accident led the people of Alton to begin

The Alton Bus Crash

Picture of the current intersection where the accident occurred. *Photo by author.*

pressuring their local authorities to do something about this hazard. One Alton resident described the pit as "a man-made hazard that had been around so long that it was taken for granted as a natural hazard." Hidalgo County officials' response was to point out to the residents that it was the state that had the authority to make improvements to the road in question, and so the state would need to be the one to put forth a bill to build a barrier. Accordingly, Texas State Representative Juan Hinojosa (Democrat out of nearby McAllen, Texas) did attempt to introduce a bill on this important issue, but it never made it out of the House.[27] Unfortunately, like other serious yet unaddressed issues, it would take an unimaginable calamity to finally force authorities and legislators into action.

Shortly after picking up his last two passengers, Gilberto Pena took bus no. 6 onto FM 676, his passengers talking and laughing and some of them looking out the window. These students could see the fast approach of the Dr Pepper truck.[28] In the truck, Ruben Perez was traveling north on Bryan Road toward FM 676. According to his testimony to the National Transportation Safety Board (NTSB), this was the farthest north he had ever been on this particular road. The upcoming stop sign at the intersection with FM 676 was slightly bent, and Perez testified that it was also covered by the leaves and branches of a tree, preventing him from seeing it. As he approached the stop sign at forty-five miles per hour, his assistant, Ruben Pena, warned him that there was a stop sign up ahead.[29] Pena would later state to the court at Ruben Perez's trial, "As we were getting close to the stop sign, I noticed some yellow to the right." He yelled in Spanish to Ruben to "watch out." "When we got closer I noticed the yellow was a school bus, that's when we collided."[30] He was not the only one to see a collision about to unfold.

Virginia pointed out that even she and her schoolmates could see the truck approaching the stop sign at a high rate of speed and came to the frightening realization that it was going too fast to stop.[31] Some of the students who witnessed the truck speeding toward the stop sign yelled warnings to the bus driver, who immediately began to brake and turn to the right in a desperate attempt to avoid the collision. One can only imagine the bus driver's state of mind knowing that sitting behind him and relying solely on him for their safety were eighty-one young souls.

Too often, bus drivers are faceless in their communities, but to the student who climbs up the steps to get into the bus, he or she is the first face they see as they transform from just being a kid to being a student at a school. They are the first school representatives the children see and the last at the end of the year. In some regards, the driver knows aspects of the students' lives that no educator ever sees, like the home they leave and go back to at the end of the day. It was especially true for these students, who came from a neighborhood where some did not have a floor in their homes or indoor plumbing.[32] Yet these kids went to school every weekday and made it through the day, in a well-lit environment where one could go to the bathroom indoors and experience what it's like to have air conditioning in a hot and humid environment like that of the Valley. The bus driver knows all of this, and in the knowing comes the weight of responsibility, something that weighed heavily on Gilberto Pena.

Perez's Dr Pepper truck was three hundred feet away when his assistant's warning forced him into action. He began to apply his truck's brakes (he testified that the breaks did not work when he applied them) and then the semi-trailer's brake valve. He then began to downshift his vehicle in an attempt to avoid the accident.[33] Both the bus and the truck driver's last-minute actions would not be enough to prevent the disaster. Edna Ortiz (a survivor) could see the bus driver from her seat. She stated, "Everyone was screaming as the bus headed into the caliche pit which we all knew was full of water. As the bus was falling, I looked at the bus driver and saw his face had turned white."[34] This was his route, and he knew exactly what the students knew—the pit was large and filled with water, the equivalent of falling into a lake.

The initial impact came at the left front of the bus and the right front of the truck. The impact was so hard that it sent Ruben Perez into his

The Alton Bus Crash

assistant's side of the cab, crashing into his loader and leaving no one in control of the truck. The bus driver momentarily lost control of the vehicle because he had violently hit his head on the window. Pena quickly attempted to regain control of the bus, but just as he did, there came a second and more powerful impact. This impact came when the heavy trailer (it was full, as Perez and Pena had only made one stop, and this certainly contributed to the force the impact had on the bus) swung to the side and hit the bus on the left side as well. The Dr Pepper truck finally came to a stop alongside the shoulder of FM 676. The bus careened into the stop sign on the northern corner of FM 676 and then hit a small dirt embankment (which acted almost like a ramp for the bus) of about two feet, sending it over into the watery caliche pit, a twenty-four-foot fall. The NTSB report noted, "A witness and several students stated that before coming to final rest the school bus tilted on its left wheels and 'bobbed up' before it completely sank into the water."[35]

Virginia Flores stated, "When the bus flew up, yes, I flew up and hit the back of my head on the roof of the bus. I was flying in there like a rag doll. It seemed like in slow motion, like I saw the sky. I saw the wall, and then I saw the water, you know, and then it was like, boom, it went just like that."[36] Fellow survivor Alex De Leon also stated that when the bus went up in the air, there was complete silence inside the bus, and time seem to take longer. It was like they were in the air for longer than they were.[37] It was as if the air had been sucked out of the bus and everyone froze in terror.

Psychologist Marc Wittmann explained that the reason people feel that time slows down during a stressful or dangerous situation is due to the body's "fight or flight" response. When the body is in danger, the brain accelerates its thought process. This acceleration is not normal to the individual, who now sees the world functioning more slowly than usual, but this is only a perception. This enhanced perception allows for the individual to attempt to "fight" or "flee" from the situation.[38] However, neither fight nor flight was an option for those aboard bus no. 6, but they knew where the bus was headed and what was in store for them. As the bus plunged into the water, it carried brothers and sisters, cousins, friends and acquaintances. In the end, they would all be bonded by tragedy, a bond and scar they carry to this day.

Another student who would be forever bound to this tragic event was young Perla Alanec, who was just seventeen years old at the time of the accident. That day, she had missed the bus and was chasing after it when she witnessed the collision between the beverage truck and the school bus. She stated, "The bus rolled over and went into the water."[39] Perla would later be called on to help the National Transportation Safety Board (NTSB) re-create the accident for its investigation. The NTSB report described the accident as follows:

> *The school bus continued in a northwest direction and dropped approximately 24 feet into a caliche pit (excavation pit) partially filled with water, located in the northwest corner of the intersection. The bus came to rest on its left side facing southeast, totally submerged in approximately 10 feet of water, approximately 35 feet from the nearest shoreline. The bus front boarding door was jammed shut, but the rear emergency exit door was operable. No other emergency exits were on the bus.*[40]

The fact that the report stated that the "rear emergency exit door was operable" did not necessarily mean it was an easy method of escape for the students. The bus landed on its left side. This placed the emergency door, which swings out, submerged in the water. Therefore, the students had to struggle with the weight of the water pressure to get the door open. This difficult prospect added to the chaotic scene inside the bus as described by survivors. The passengers of bus no. 6 hardly knew what had happened. Survivor Marisele Ortega, fifteen, talking from her hospital bed, declared, "I don't know what happened. I was in the bus and it rolled over into the water. Nobody screamed, nobody knew what was happening." Indeed, Ortega's words give testament to the swiftness of the events.[41] Not only did the events happen quickly, but the muddy quality of the water also lent itself to the confusion and disorientation. First, the bus flew through the air. Flores described seeing "the sky, I saw the wall, and then I saw the water." The dizzying nature of the fall, coupled with the murkiness of the water, made for a loss of sense of direction, hampering escape.[42]

Jesus Cuellar described the content of the water as "dirty, ugly, filthy," and it quickly filled the bus. "We couldn't see anything and at the time all of us were crammed up on each other." Some seats had broken off the bus and added to the objects and people floating inside the bus.[43] Struggling with the rear exit was simply not an option for the eighty-one passengers with children drowning and seconds counting. The passengers were left with only one other option: the small windows on the sides of the bus. The regular openings were insufficient for most of the passengers to fit through them. Many windows were broken, and those who found the windows and could fit through the small openings swam through them.[44] With only the small windows as a means of escape, the situation was precarious, with eighty-one people all struggling to find which way was out, unable to see anything and panicking as the precious air in their lungs was dwindling.

Alex De Leon described the scene inside:

> *I remember the bus going down into the water and it had nosedived, and all the screaming stopped for about two seconds. As we waited for the bus to see what side it was going to turn, we all looked at each other like, "What was happening?" Then the water began to come in through the front windshield. We looked at each other still trying to see which way to go when all of a sudden the bus went to its left side. That's when more water began to fill the bus much faster, and everyone was scrambling to get out. It was then that I remembered that my sister sat on the left side of the bus and I was on the right side. When the bus hit, I saw her fly over her seat and I remember we looked at each other and when the bus went sideways I grabbed her and picked her up and put her over the side window. By that point, the water was up to my knees, and I pulled myself out as well. When I got out, all I could hear was yelling all around; it was complete chaos. I saw people looking down towards the windows as we were walking on top of the side of the bus. You could see people trying to get out, but in those days the windows had these clasps and you had to put your hands on them and snap them at the same time. It would snap and lock if you did not pull them all the way down. So you had to make sure you pulled them the right way, which was extremely difficult because by that point the bus was completely full of water. I and my friends did our best to pull who we could from the open windows. I could see everyone struggling to help. Once we were out, we were struggling to figure out what to do as we stood on the bus wondering where to go.*[45]

Those who made it to the surface desperately tried to pull their fellow classmates from the bus. They reached into the murky waters, pulling at anyone they could feel and getting them out from the bus through the windows.[46] The school bus driver, Gilberto Pena, injured and bloody, was credited with pulling many of the children to safety. By the time rescuers made it to him, he was shaking, wet and covered in mud and blood. He was running on desperation and adrenaline and a profound sense of duty to the responsibility he had to the children and their parents.[47]

Cindy Cantu managed to save her best friend, Estela Flores, after Cindy was rescued by a boy who lived just across the street from her. She was so involved in studying for a test that was coming up that day that she did not

The Accident

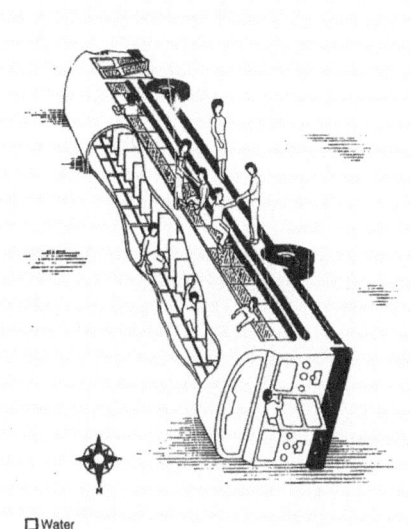

Figure 3.--Illustration representing how some of the students reported escaping from the submerged school bus. The illustration is based on the condition of the bus when it was examined by the Safety Board. Only a few students are shown for illustrative purposes.

☐ Water

NTSB illustration of students escaping from the bus. *Courtesy of the National Transportation Board Accident Report HAR-90-02.*

see the accident coming but was keenly aware of it with the first impact of the truck on the bus. She was seated with Estela, but once they landed and the bus came to rest on its side (the side she and her best friend were seated on), she lost her friend in the rush of water. At first, she thought she was about to die, but then her heroic neighbor pulled her out. In turn, she began to help pull more people out from the bus when she saw her best friend, struggling. She focused all of her strength on pulling Estela out from the water. However, by the time she pulled her friend out from the bus, she had stopped breathing. Undeterred, Cindy quickly began CPR on Estela's lifeless body. After a few scary moments, Estela began to breathe on her own and opened her eyes.[48] This would be one of many instances of friends saving friends and siblings saving siblings from the muddy waters.

Some rescue attempts did not have successful outcomes. As some of the students were attempting to pull others from the bus, those rescuers were pulled back into the water by other submerged students, desperately grasping at anything in attempt to escape. As a result, they drowned together.[49] Tragically, some who went back into the bus to rescue family or friends never came back up.[50] Many of those who managed to make it through the murky waters and out through the window would later be struck with survivor's guilt, thinking that perhaps in struggling to make their way out they may have inadvertently pushed others deeper into the abyss, people who drowned as a result of their actions.[51]

One especially devastating incident in which someone went back in and never came back involved young Mike Saenz, age fourteen. Both Mike and his brother were passengers on bus no. 6. According to witnesses, Mike managed to make it out of the dirty waters of the caliche pit to the surface and onto the side of the bus. This is where those who initially made it out of the bus stopped because the side of the bus was only a few inches from the surface, and one could stand on it and rest after the struggle to the surface. However, Mike surmised that his younger brother, David, was still inside the bus, and he dove back in to rescue him. He never returned to the surface. As pointed out by an article in *The Monitor*, "Brother's Love Led to His Death," reporter Robert Cullick wrote, "At the same time John Saenz [John had gone to school early for swimming practice] dived into the clear water of the Mission High School swimming pool in before-school practice Thursday morning, his 14-year-old brother Mike, dived purposefully into the deadly, murky waters of a caliche pit looking for their youngest brother, David." Tragically, the Saenz family lost two of their boys to the waters of the caliche pit.[52] Losing one child is unimaginable, but losing two must be soul crushing.

Others did make it out and were able to rescue some of their classmates. One individual was Eddie Vasquez. In an interview for the local newspaper, *The Monitor*, he described how he attempted to rescue others: "You felt heads and bodies and you just picked the one closest to you….I could not see nothing it was pitch dark." The fact that it was so dark inside the bus, even though the side of the bus was exposed to the sunlight, demonstrates just how dirty, muddy and disorientating the water in the caliche pit was. Shortly after they hit the water, he looked for his siblings, Alberto (twelve) and Veronica (sixteen). The article noted:

> *Eddie Vasquez said he pulled three people from the bus. Two of those died, including Yesenia Perez, a 15-year-old from Mission who died at 10:40 a.m. Friday* [the twentieth victim]. *"She was the last person I took out," Vasquez said. "All those people, I thought they were dead because they were purple and swollen."*[53]

It would not be until later in the day that Eddie discovered he had lost the siblings he was struggling to find.

The Accident

An outside rescue effort began almost immediately after the accident. All the nearby residents heard the crash, and some came running to the scene, desperate to save the children. Roque Sosa, who lived across the street from the pit, lowered a triple length of water hose into the pit in an attempt to pull the survivors out. Many of the children had managed to swim the fifteen feet to the sheer sides of the pit and were clinging desperately to it, calling for help.[54]

Alex De Leon was the first person who made it to Mr. Sosa's water hose. Mr. Sosa recognized Alex as one of the neighborhood boys whom he would pay to help him break the horses. He yelled down to him, "Alex, Alex!" When Alex looked up, he could make out Roque at the edge of the caliche pit. He then saw him throw down what he thought was a rope, but it was the water hose. "*Nada para acá*" ("swim here"), he directed. Alex decided to give it a try to swim for it. When he got to the hose, he began to be pulled up and was surprised with how strong Mr. Sosa was because he was being pulled up pretty fast. When he got to the top, he was greeted with the sight of Mr. Sosa seated on top of a horse, with the hose tied to it, and he realized that is how he was able to pull him up so fast.[55] The fact that Mr. Sosa was able to recognize what had happened, was able to get a long enough water hose, mount his horse and get to the edge in time to be one of the first rescuers to the scene makes Roque one of the unsung heroes of the whole disaster. His quick thinking and ingenuity saved lives that day.

Roque Sosa also was witness to the arrival of parents, stating, "I could see the mothers of the rest of the kids (still in the bus) trying to save them, but it was too late."[56] Perla Alanec also witnessed four men dive into the water, helping to pull children from the bus.[57]

One parent actually witnessed her own child, who was in the crash, involved in the rescue effort. Ms. Elvira Ortiz's daughter, Edna, was the last student to board the bus. They lived just across the street from the pickup area, so Elvira heard the initial impact of the Dr Pepper truck on the bus. Her thoughts immediately ran to her daughter. With her heart pounding and fear racing through her veins, she raced out the front door of the house. Once outside, she was startled to be greeted by the image of the truck, damaged and stopped on the side of the road, with the bus nowhere to be seen. She ran into the street, and a man in a car passing by offered her a ride to a pay phone so she could call for help. With the call made, he drove her back to the scene of the accident. She arrived at the scene and began to panic, her heart beating through her chest as she could not see Edna. Then she saw her muddy face coming out one of the bus's windows and was

The Alton Bus Crash

Artist Estrella Garcia's depiction of the aerial view of the accident site. *Courtesy of the artist.*

instantly relieved. However, she once again began to fear for her daughter's life as she watched her go back in to rescue other trapped students. Edna was later removed from the scene, her body covered in scratches from other students attempting to claw their way to safety.[58]

The desperation of neighbors, especially parents, who were anxious to help because they could see the horrific accident scene and hear the screaming of the desperate children, was an added aspect to the rescue effort that authorities would have to deal with as they attempted to coordinate a multifaceted and multi-agency response. This was something no one had planned for, but everyone wanted to reach out and lend a hand, especially because time was of the essence. However, this also meant that it would be difficult to control the scene because as they arrived, there were already neighbors and parents doing their best to help. Unfortunately for some, it was already too late. One of the witnesses on the scene reported seeing one of the mothers collapse to the ground from grief, and she had to be transported to the hospital.[59] Indeed, for many at the scene, the sounds and the sights would be too much to bear, scarring witness and family members for life.

The Accident

OUTSIDE THE BUS

As chaotic as the events were that unfolded inside the bus, the events outside were just as bad and, sadly, just as heart-rending. To completely understand the community's and parents' responses to the accident, one must first place himself or herself in the time and place at which it occurred. First, there were no such things as social media, the internet or smartphones. Although cellphones did exist, they were only beginning to be introduced in that area, and given the fact that the area comprised mostly low-income residents, many of them did not even have a house phone let alone a cellphone. In the present, if something were to happen in a school, some sort of tragedy, the parents would probably hear about it from their children via cellphone, as we have seen in mass shootings and other contemporary tragedies. However, at the time of the Alton Bus Crash, parents found out if they personally heard the wreck (which some did) or heard the sirens of the first responders or if someone went to their doorstep and told them what happened. One can only imagine the panic of parents running or driving to the pit, hospital or school in a desperate attempt to find their children. As far as emergency-response crews, they arrived as quickly as they could with what they could, and as the word spread out, neighboring emergency crews from different cities came to the scene, as did members of the Texas Department of Public Safety and Border Patrol. For that one moment, they were all parents trying to save the children.

One cannot understate the involvement of residents who lived near the accident site. They either saw or heard the crash and went running to see what happened and what they could do to help. Family members who made it to the pit jumped in to rescue their loved ones before authorities could stop them. Lupina (fourteen) and Apolonia Regalado's (thirteen) older brother, Pedro, heard the crash from their home and bolted to the scene. He dove into the cold, murky waters searching for his sisters. He managed to find Apolonia, but she was unconscious and not breathing. Pedro desperately began to administer CPR, but his efforts garnered no response from his little sister. Hers would be one of the twenty-one names that ended up on the memorial at the site of the accident. Next, he was able to find Lupina, who was still breathing by the time he found her, but she would later also succumb to her injuries. The Regalados would be one of the two families who would lose two children to the accident, an almost unbearable cross to bear.[60]

The Alton Bus Crash

Artist Estrella Garcia's depiction of rescue workers standing on the bus. *Courtesy of the artist.*

According to Lupina and Apolonia's older sister, Maria, the girls had done something that struck everyone as odd that morning—even more so after the events of that day. They went back into their mother's room twice to kiss her and tell her goodbye before they left. Maria also described the girls as very attached to their mother, constantly showering her with attention, braiding her hair and applying her makeup for her. Lupina's death was even more significant due to the fact that she was going to turn fifteen the week after the accident and was preparing for her *quinceañera*. A *quinceañera* in Mexican culture is a coming-of-age party for a fifteen-year-old young lady. The event is something close to a wedding in the amount of money that can be spent on it. The dress, like that of a wedding or a prom dress, is the center of the celebration. Lupina had already purchased and been fitted for it, and she was super excited for her big day.[61]

The official rescue effort came from myriad state, local and federal agencies, ranging from the Alton Volunteer Firefighters to local and state police, the Hidalgo County sheriff and Border Patrol officers from the nearby McAllen office. Volunteer firefighters Raul Garcia and Jose Solis were among the first rescuers to arrive at the scene. Upon their arrival, they found "two dozen bloodied students standing on the bus crying for help; however, the ladder the rescuers had in their possession would only reach to the water's edge of the pit, not to the bus itself."[62] Consequently, the two men had to swim back and forth to bring the children to safety. During his rescue attempts, Garcia bore witness to many of the children who were already purple and lifeless inside the bus. Indeed, many at the site could see the last air bubbles escaping from the dying victims.[63] Some of the rescuers felt guilty for not being able to save more, but as Fire Chief Omar Botello stated, "My men, they feel guilty. They wanted to be able to do more. They did all that they could do. They feel guilty because they wanted to save all of the lives."

The Accident

Larry W. Clubb/Monitor File Photo
Rescuers work to save children from a sunken bus after it collided with a Dr Pepper truck, sending the bus into a nearby caliche pit in this file photo from Sept. 21, 1989.

The Monitor newspaper photo of the rescue effort. *From* The Monitor, *September 22, 2004.*

For only twenty-one to die out of eighty-one, under the conditions in which the accident occurred, was a miracle in and of itself.[64] Yet for the men and women who choose a career in emergency services, the loss of even one, especially a child, is one of the most difficult aspects of the job. It would be something the rescuers would deal with for the rest of their lives.

One man who was also one of the initial rescuers to arrive at the scene was Luis Guerrero. His heroic efforts earned him national media exposure. He was a volunteer firefighter for the City of Alton. He lived half a mile from the caliche pit. Guerrero heard about the accident on his police scanner and immediately made his way to the site.[65] He arrived at the scene to discover that twenty students had already made their way out of the bus. Guerrero noted, "I jumped about 30 feet down into water and I started getting kids out of the windows." He found the students in various conditions. "I got some of them back breathing again and I pulled another couple of kids out. Then some other help started coming in." However, he kept going back to rescue as many as he could. As word of the accident made its way through the small community, crowds gathered at the top of the pit. Guerrero recalled, "People started calling my name out [a sign of how small Alton was that Luis Guerrero was instantly recognized by those at the top of the pit], and I looked and I saw a lot of people all over the place. And they said, 'Luis look for my kid....Luis my daughter is missing.'"

The cries from above only urged Luis on to continue his rescue efforts. He ran from window to window, reaching in, grabbing and pulling at what he could find—a hand, hair, a limb—and he would pull them out, administering what aid he could and getting them to safety. Guerrero found that the bus driver, Gilberto Pena, was also rescuing children despite his injuries. Guerrero noted, "The bus driver was trying to help me, but he was injured. His head was busted open. I just told him to stay calm." Luis encountered two students he could not revive. "I tried to pump their stomach and there was no response." In total, Guerrero completed ten dives, but after the tenth, all the dirty water he swallowed and the fact that he had banged his head on the bus finally caught up to him, and he collapsed to the ground. Emergency medical personnel treated him at the site and took him to Rio Grande Regional Hospital in the nearby city of McAllen, where his stomach had to be pumped to get rid of the filthy water of the caliche pit.[66] In his ten dives, Guerrero actually managed to perform CPR on four victims and successfully revive them. He was interviewed by *Good Morning America* in which he declared that in his year and a half as a volunteer firefighter, "I've never seen anything like this before. It was terrible." He credited the efforts of all the rescue workers, volunteers and bystanders who assisted that day. If not for them, there would certainly have been more loss of life that fateful day.[67]

Indeed, scuba diver Al Nye pointed out, "We had to break the glass of the windows to get in."[68] Nye was driving his own kids to school when the accident occurred. He stated that the water so murky "you couldn't see at all in there." Like all the others, his efforts were guided more by touch than by any visual input. He was able to pull seven bodies from the bus[69]—a remarkable number under the circumstances but a demonstration of how many students were trapped in the bus and how quickly the rescuers were able to make it to the area of the accident.

The dark and dirty waters the students and rescuers had to deal with became a concern for healthcare officials. Broad-spectrum antibiotics

The Accident

A *Progress Times* photo of the bus in the water. *From the* Progress Times, *September 27, 1989.*

began to be given to rescue workers and students the Friday after the accident. These were done as an initial protective measure until the results of lab work done on them came back, and they could then administer more appropriate antibiotics. The water in the pit was stagnant. It was also contaminated with human waste as well as the diesel fuel from the bus. To this day, the pit still receives runoff water from various sources.[70] In fact, over the course of the weekend, several students were admitted into the hospital from complications due to their swallowing and inhaling the water.[71]

As the rescue efforts were unfolding, the kids' first thoughts were to race to help their friends and siblings, and then their next thoughts were of their parents. The minute Alex De Leon was pulled from the pit by Roque Sosa, his first thought (knowing that his sister was safe on top of the bus) was his mother. Alex arrived at the surface and turned his head in the direction of his home, which was not too far away, and as he began to move toward it, he was stopped by a Border Patrolman, who had arrived at the scene and told him to wait there at the scene. He paused and then ran past him, as fast he could, all the way home. His only thought was to get to his mother and let her know what had happened. He got to the front door and began banging on it, yelling for his mother.[72]

The Alton Bus Crash

His mother, Virginia Ruiz, stumbled out of bed when she heard the commotion at the front door. She opened it, and there was Alex, standing before her in drenched and mussy clothes. He was crying; the tears were streaming down, leaving clear trails down his muddy face. He sobbingly told his mother that the bus had crashed into the water and that they had to go there. "Where is your sister?" Ms. Ruiz asked. "She's on top of the bus!" Alex responded, exasperated, still catching his breath, with the adrenaline still coursing through his veins. It took Virginia a moment to take it all in, then she had Alex help her with his two little sisters to get them into the car. She looked to the canal that ran behind the house and asked, "Where is the bus?" "It's in the pit," Alex responded. "What pit?" Ms. Ruiz questioned. While they drove south in the direction of the pit, Ms. Ruiz kept looking toward the canal in search of the bus. As they got to the end of the road near the pit, she stopped the car when Alex said, "There!" pointing toward the caliche pit.[73]

The sight she came upon was one that would remain in her mind for the rest of her life. It was complete chaos, with papers and other debris scattered all around. She looked down into the pit and could see the bus lying on its side, submerged in water, and students standing on top of it, attempting to pull others out from the submerged bus. She felt goosebumps all over her body as she watched the scene unfold. She was frozen, trying to think what she could do to help. She had one child in her arms, and Alex had the other. She told Alex to take them and put them in the car, away from all the chaos, so they would not have to bear witness to the tragedy unraveling around them. She tried to find a way to get down to help, to find her daughter, but Alex stopped her, telling her that there was no way down there. She then saw a group of men walking toward her with her daughter, wet and covered in mud. She was holding her arm, and her nose was bloody. She had broken both her wrist and nose from the crash.[74]

"Mom! Mom!" Alex called to her as the family was reunited. "Mom, do you remember my friend Roman?" "Yes, he's your best friend." Virginia replied. Alex began crying and after a moment said, "Well, he's dead. I couldn't get him out! I got some of the people out, but I couldn't get him!" He looked at her with despair. Here was a young boy coming to the reality of death for the first time, the death of someone he had grown up with, played with and confided in. These feelings were echoed from all those who lost someone that day, friend or relative. Ms. Ruiz felt for her son but was glad that her children were safe. Her husband found them by the edge of the pit. He was one of the Border Patrolmen in the boats assisting with the rescue. He asked if everyone was okay. She said the girls were in the car, but they had to go to the hospital because of Virginia's injuries. He offered to go home and watch the little ones while she went to the hospital with Alex and Virginia (she was referred to by the family as Virginia Jr.).[75]

The entire scene was surreal for all present. There were all kinds of people and vehicles representing federal, state, county and local authorities. There were mothers screaming down into the pit, calling their children's names. Some were being held back from jumping by family members and law enforcement. Former KRGV Channel 5 reporter Randy Eilts described the scene:

> *When we got to the scene, there was sheriff's deputies, D.P.S. [Texas Department of Public Safety]. There was just people all over the place and ambulances arriving from all directions and cities. The first thing I thought when I got there was, "Where was the school bus?" So I looked around and went over the pit, and that's when the reality of the situation dawned on me. The school bus was under water. We immediately began to become part of the chaos trying to get the camera set up and rolling. I remember standing there on the edge and looking down, watching the rescue effort still frantically occurring and then turning around and looking behind to see screaming and crying parents. I remember one woman on her knees with her hands up in the air screaming and another lady being held back by her husband. Then I went into reporter mode, getting shots and looking for someone in charge, that appeared to be a D.P.S. officer who I asked how many victims had been transported to the hospital. At first it was eight, and I would check in every ten to fifteen minutes and the number kept growing. After a bit of being on scene, I realized that the boats were bringing bodies back from the bus and placing them on the other side of the pit to have them away from the scene of the accident. There was a growing line of bodies under a yellow tarp, and it was at that point I realized just how young these kids were.*[76]

Another KRGV Channel 5 reporter, Sandra Quintanilla, also arrived on the scene and was assigned to a temporary morgue that had been set up at a county pavilion on Schuepbach Road. Parents would go there to identify their child, and then the child would be transferred to a funeral home.[77] When at the scene, she had the difficult job of interviewing parents who went to the pavilion seeking information about their child or children. Ms. Quintanilla stated:

The Alton Bus Crash

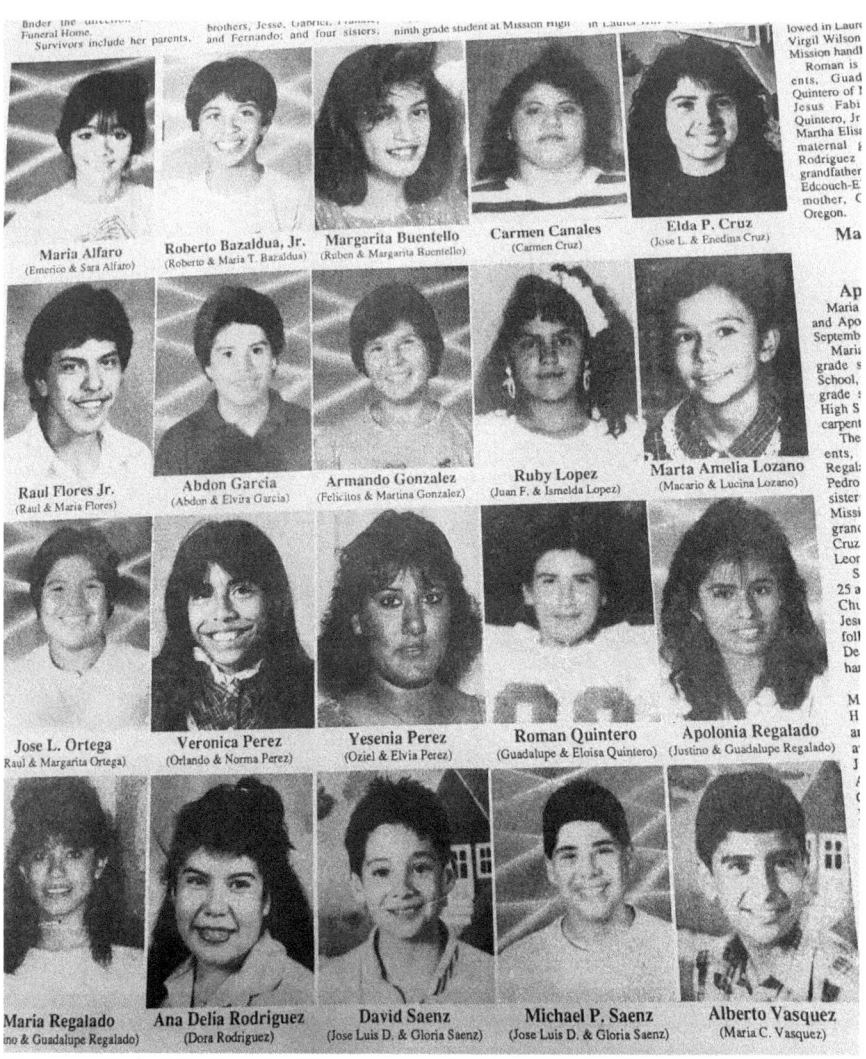

A *Progress Times* photo of twenty of the twenty children who were lost as a result of the accident. *From the* Progress Times, *September 27, 1989.*

> *I saw so many people that were completely distraught, and I really felt bad about the job I was there to do. I walked with the microphone over to a lady I saw standing there and began to interview her. She was telling me that she was looking for two of her kids, but she had not been able to get any information about their whereabouts. I remember that we aired that portion of the interview on the air, and later on I came to find out that she had lost both the children. That moment will forever remain in my heart.*[78]

The woman she interviewed was Ms. Saenz, who lost two of her children while her other boy was at swim practice.

Nineteen students perished at the site of the accident, with forty taken to Mission Regional Hospital (the hospital closest to the accident scene) and seven to Rio Grande Regional Hospital and eighteen to McAllen Medical Center, the latter hospitals being across the street from each other in the nearby city of McAllen.[79] A survivor standing wet and shirtless spoke to a reporter and pointed out that most of the children who died were the smaller ones, who could not force or break the windows open as he and others did. He stated that the bus filled with water in fifteen seconds and that they pulled out who they could in that small amount of time.[80] Of the nineteen who died on the scene, thirteen of them were middle school students (the youngest group on board).[81] Three more students would die in the days following the accident, with Elizabeth Flores (fifteen) being the last, dying from cardiac arrest (due to complications of injuries suffered in the accident) on Friday, September 29.[82] In the end, the twenty-one victims would forever link the city of Alton with the dubious distinction of being the location of the "worst school bus accident in Texas history."

COMMUNITY

The response from the community was immense. To begin with, in order to deal with such a large loss of life in a small community like Alton, counselors were sent from nearby school districts and the Red Cross. These mental health professionals arrived at the Mission schools and went as far as traveling door to door throughout Alton, offering assistance to any and all who asked for it at no charge to the residents.[83] Monetary, food and clothing donations also arrived from the people of the Rio Grande Valley and beyond. In addition, in response to the request of Mission mayor Pat Townsend, drivers in the Valley drove with their lights on.[84] Continental Airlines, which flies out of the neighboring city of McAllen, sponsored a giveaway of five hundred round-trip tickets to London that netted $50,000 for the victims of the tragedy.[85] So much money was coming in to help the victims and families that Alton mayor San Juanita Zamora appointed a committee to control and distribute the funds.[86] As one phase of its initial response, Valley Coca-Cola Corporation paid all the victims' medical bills and for the funerals of those who died from the accident.[87]

The Alton Bus Crash

The front of Valley Coca-Cola Bottling Company. *Photo by author.*

Concerning the response from Valley Coca-Cola, Ms. Julie Martinez, spokesperson for the company, became the go-to person throughout the entire affair because she was the only one in management who spoke Spanish. Therefore, she could communicate with the victims and their families. She was given a checkbook and a logbook and set up an office in Alton. The corporate office was in nearby McAllen. She was instructed to write out checks for whatever the victims and family members needed and to keep a log of everything she was paying out. The logbook contained lines for whom the money was made out to, how much the check was for and what it was going to be used for. The only caveat was that she could not make any payments to someone who had already retained legal counsel.[88]

The logbook reveals payments and notations for all manner of items. There were payments made out for funeral clothes for one of the children, jewelry lost in the accident and ongoing medical bills. These bills were not just for the physical health of the children but also the mental health of victims. One claim paid out to Carlota Castilla was for her daughter to see McAllen psychiatrist Dr. Igoa, because although she was not in the accident, her friends and relatives were and she was scared to go to school or ride the bus. Some people came in seeking help buying groceries and new school supplies and paying utility bills and rent. Others sought out assistance for the loss of wages that resulted from them taking time off from work to deal with the accident (like many in the area and beyond, a majority of the people of Alton lived paycheck to paycheck, and taking time off for the tragedy, hospital stays and doctors' visits took a major toll on the family's finances).

The Accident

Another frequently noted expense was money to help family members who did not live nearby travel down to South Texas for the funerals and just to be with their family members to offer them support.[89] These were paid out and documented by Ms. Martinez, who for the time and for the family members became the face of Valley Coca-Cola.

Valley Coca-Cola Bottling Company as a corporate entity made the following decisions upon hearing of the accident. First it ceased all advertisements in the area and then issued the following statement:

> *We deeply regret the tragedy that took place this morning in Alton, Texas involving a school bus and one of our delivery trucks. We express our condolences to the families and friends of the children that have drowned or been injured as a result of the accident.*
>
> *We are fully cooperating in the investigation of this incident with the local and state authorities and have no further comments to make at this time.*[90]

The company would also institute a blood drive at its facility in which forty employees sat to donate blood through the United Blood Services. Coca-Cola also made a deal with Charter Palms, a local mental health facility, and gave it what was in a sense a "blank check" to treat victims and their families with whatever they might need.[91] The company's legal team was brought down, and meetings were set up with Mission mayor Pat Townsend and Mission Schools superintendent Ralph Cantu.[92] The company knew just how serious the incident was and the huge potential for litigation it was facing, not to mention damage to its label and reputation, so it attempted to mitigate any potential damage.

In addition to the details already mentioned, there was also the emotional and spiritual support that poured out from the community. Most funerals were so crowded with mourners and supporters that there were lines to get in.[93] The funerals for four of the victims—Martha Lozano, thirteen; Carmen Canales, seventeen; and two cousins, Veronica and Yesenia Perez, fourteen and fifteen—were held at the large church at the Shrine of Our Lady of Guadalupe in San Juan, Texas. This would be the first funeral ever held at the shrine, a testament to the gravity of the loss that the Valley community experienced.[94] The mass was attended by more than five thousand people and was filled with the wails and cries of the families of the victims as the priest preached for togetherness and called for the members of the community to support one another through these difficult times.[95]

Relatives of the 21 children gather at the front of the church to be blessed and pray at Mass at the San Martín de Porres Catholic Church in Alton Tuesday night.

The Monitor newspaper photo of families gathered to mourn in San Martin De Porres Catholic Church. *From* The Monitor, *September 22, 1999.*

One group of people who reached out to the community was a group out of Kansas that had a deep, personal understanding of what the Alton families were experiencing. They were members of the First Assemblies of God Church from Radcliffe, Kentucky. These parishioners were still recovering from their own on tragedy on May 14, 1988, in which twenty-seven people were killed (twenty-four children and three adults) when a bus was struck by a drunk driver driving on the wrong side of the road. The impact in the front of the bus ignited the gas tank, which eliminated the front door as a means of escape. Most of those who were killed were seated in the front of the bus. One body was found holding the fire extinguisher.[96] The parishioners reached out with sympathetic words to the Alton families, donations and offers to help in any way they could. One of the parishioners was quoted as saying, "We feel their loss as though it was our very own."[97] The loss of a child is a collective experience in the sense that it is the fear of every parent in the world, and hearing of the loss of even one child is enough to make a parent take a moment and feel that despair. In the case of these families from Kentucky and Alton, it was not only a sympathetic thought, it was the flood of memories and emotions that are invoked when the memories of their tragedy are brought forth with the news of others experiencing a similar calamity.

The emotional state of the survivors and those directly and indirectly affected was what the Valley community focused on. Organizations like the Salvation Army and the American Red Cross responded to the crisis. The Red Cross established an assistance center first at the Mission Community Center and then later at Alton Elementary School. Family members and victims went to this center to receive information, supplies and counseling; it was a place where people who wanted to volunteer to help could go and assist with directing families to the appropriate individual or agency. They put together donations such as food, clothing and school supplies into care packages for the families. In the end, more than two hundred people arrived at the center, from homemakers to doctors. People from all walks of life stepped up to serve their community in its time of need.[98]

Additionally, more than twenty students attending University of Texas Pan American (today University of Texas Rio Grande Valley) in nearby Edinburg, Texas, majoring in social work arrived to help out and bring their training into the real world. They spoke to the victims and gave them the opportunity to express their grief and guided them toward further assistance.[99] The need to allow someone to talk about their experience is pointed out by McAllen psychiatrist Dr. Igoa (who was one of the two psychiatrists treating the victims): "Those involved must be provided with a 'debriefing' a time to process what happened and their feelings about the accident. They need a supportive environment where they can express their feelings, concerns and fears."[100] He added that in order to prevent a delayed reaction, support must be rendered as soon as possible. An additional concern would be that of survivor's guilt, which can manifest itself in different ways.[101] It could be the guilt that comes from the knowledge that you lived and your friends or loved ones did not, especially when it can be due to something as random as where you were sitting on the bus. It can also be the parent who placed them on the bus. Perhaps this was the one day they did not drive them to school, or maybe it was, "I wish I had taught them to swim." It can also manifest itself in a student who did not take the bus or missed it that day. Without a doubt, this calamity reached all the members of that small community who were intimately connected with one another.

SCHOOL

In time, these children/students had to return to school, a school that would now seem foreign, without familiar faces and filled with the fear and anxiety of the haunting tragedy hanging over their heads. The Friday of the week of the accident, classes were canceled and a huge community event was planned. The memorial service was held in the neighboring community of Mission. More than nine thousand people attended the service at Tom Landry Stadium, which had preempted the football game between Mission and Brownsville Pace High Schools. Among the attending were priests from more than thirteen parishes from across the Valley, politicians and various public officials. Speeches were presented in both English and Spanish for the largely Mexican American population, and a poem written by three girls from Mission's sister school district of La Joya was read:

> *The age of those departed is so hard to comprehend.*
> *Tragedy and disaster—Why was their innocence condemned?*
> *There's a reason for it all, yet man cannot understand.*
> *For this we join together and extend a helping hand.*[102]

Also present at the memorial were fourteen flower wreaths representing schools and individuals from Texas to California. During the memorial, a fascinating event occurred: balloons were released into the air after the names of the twenty-one dead students were called. The balloons all somehow gathered together in the middle of the field, and once the names were all read, they floated off into the sky together. It was this odd occurrence that assured some of the observers of the final destination of the souls of the children—they were all there together forever, children, friends and family.[103] Furthermore, attending and speaking at the memorial service was San Juanita Zamora, mayor of Alton, who urged her people on by stating, "We cannot forget what happened, but we must go forward with our lives."[104] For these children/students, moving forward would mean returning to school. It was the beginning of September, and the year had only just begun.

The following Monday, September 25, 1989, Mission schools reopened, but for all those touched in one way or another by the accident, it would not look or feel the same. The school district had a plan in place in order to help its students deal with this unprecedented tragedy. In fact, for many of these young children, this would be the first time in their lives that they would be touched by or deal with death on such a personal level, whether it was

THE ACCIDENT

The Monitor newspaper article on the memorial service for victims of the accident. *From* The Monitor, *September 23, 1989.*

Page two of the student newspaper the *Eagle Eye*. Courtesy of the Mission High School Library and the Mission Consolidated School District.

siblings, family or friends; this would be one of their first permanent losses. To deal with the situation, the district had counselors follow the schedule of each of the victims who died as a result of the crash and attend each of his or her classes in order to help the students with the loss of their classmate.[105]

The day of the accident, in the Mission Schools, news trickled down to the staff and students slowly. Ms. Maggie Rojas, who lost two ninth-grade students, Jose Ortega and Ana Rodriguez, described the sense of dread that made its way into her mind and that of her students. At first, during first period, they heard there was some kind of accident. Then, by second period, they began to hear that there was some loss of life; they knew that it was going to be bad, but there was always hope. Rojas recalled thinking that Ana was in band, so perhaps the reason she was not in class was that she was on a band trip, so she clung to that and just hoped that Jose was merely absent. This was the hope among the staff as they compared notes with one another as to those who were missing. What was going on? Why no announcement? Early in the day, news was trickling in by word of mouth among the staff, and no real official statement was put out early on.[106] Lack of communication and the chaos on the scene did not facilitate an accurate dissemination of information to anyone.

Consequently, the need for emotional support extended beyond the students to the staff as well. Even though it was early on in the year, the students had already made their way into the hearts of the staff, who referred to the students as their "kids." This is common among educators, who at times spend more time with their students than even their own children. Teachers, especially those who have children, make these close connections with their students as part of educating them because the only way to truly get kids to learn from you is to let them know you care about them. It is also necessary because all students learn differently, and teachers must relate to their students and learn their students' strengths and weaknesses in order to effectively provide lessons to them. This interconnectedness breeds emotional connections that sometimes last for a lifetime. As a result, when a teacher loses a student, he or she feels it on a deeply emotional level. In the case of the Alton school bus accident, multiple students can be an overwhelming burden to bear. It means an empty seat that will never again be filled with that young beautiful face whose smile can carry you through a hectic day.

For the students and parents, there was another aspect of the return to school that weighed heavily on their minds: would they be taking the bus to school? Veronica Salinas, who lost two of her close friends, began her day with giving survivor Edna Morales a ride to school. Edna had just been released from the hospital the Saturday following the accident and had persistent nightmares. She asked her friend for a ride until she felt she was emotionally ready to begin riding the bus again. For parents like Susie Ramon, it was almost inconceivable to allow their children on a bus in Alton because there were other open caliche pits in town like the one the bus had fallen into.[107] Only four of the junior high school students who were in the accident attended school, and they did not ride the bus to school. At the high school, Alex De Leon did not ride the bus either. He suffered some scrapes and bruises, but emotionally, riding a bus was out of the question.[108]

Mission High School principal Gus Zapata knew that on the day the school reopened, the absenteeism would be exceptionally high. Not everyone would be ready to return to school. However, he believed that in two to three weeks, it would return to normal because the students needed for their lives to move on, and school, their friends and after-school activities would go a long way to helping the students. Nevertheless, he knew that they would still need comfort and special treatment to allow them to reacclimate.[109] Welcoming the students back to school were maroon, white and black ribbons tied to the desks of the lost students and hugs by staff members as they made their way into the school in the mornings and into their classes. At Mission Junior High, the principal, John Abbenante, read a speech to the student body. He asked students and staff to hold hands as he read a list of the twelve students of theirs who died in the accident, referring to them as "holy innocents…who have a place reserved for them in heaven."[110] For some, the grief would be too much.

As part of their preparation for the return of the students, crisis centers were placed inside the schools, with additional counselors and priests from throughout the Valley. All through the day, emotionally overwhelmed students and staff made their way to these centers seeking comfort or to simply talk to someone. The day was far from normal. Gone from the hallways was the rambunctious banter that usually pervaded. Mission Junior High School vice-principal, Pat Gilton, described the students: "When they talk, it's in whispers. It's very, very subdued.…It's not a normal, happy, carefree day in a junior high school."[111] The low voices were like those reserved for funeral homes or funerals in general, as if it would be disrespectful to make too much noise and take away from the silence of an individual who was now gone. Also, it was hard to laugh and run around without the usual faces in the halls, and of course there was some survivor's guilt felt by many. How could one be happy? It would be weeks before things to returned to semi-normal conditions, but the 1989–90 school year would be one like no other—whether it was empty seats, fewer students taking the bus or fewer students walking across the graduation stage, nothing from that year would be the same.

As a high school teacher, I can see the lifelong friendships that students have among themselves. They have been with one another sometimes as far back as kindergarten. They have grown up with their classmates, learning, growing and becoming more social creatures, and at times those friends know more about them than their families and their siblings. Therefore, their connections are profound and cannot be discounted as simple friendships; they are much deeper than that. I have seen students be out for a week, and students will be talking about how it's not the same without them. An accident in which multiple students lose their lives can be life altering for some students, and it will be a scar that cuts so deep that they may not ever be the same person they were before. So it went for the students of Alton, walking the halls as different people from then on.

The Accident

A DARKNESS DESCENDS

Author's Note: The following description comes from my own firsthand account of what transpired the Friday after the accident when Mission High School faced Donna High School on the football field. I was a sophomore at Donna High School and a member of the marching band, which played at the game.

I first heard of the bus accident in the morning when I was in Mrs. Morales's Spanish I class. I remember one of the student office runners relayed the story to the whole class. Questions sprung up immediately, but the young girl could only repeat what she was told. The remainder of that class period, things were a little quieter, and even Mrs. Morales ceased teaching, as we all just sat and discussed what those poor students were going through. Much like the Mission schools, information was passed through word of mouth throughout the course of the day. Then we all went home to watch the news and see footage from the tragedy. The rest of the day and the week went by with some mention of the story, but not too much, until the next Friday, the day of the football game. The game would be played at Mission High School.

I was a clarinet player in the band and a member of the loading crew, which meant we loaded up all the larger instruments in the bus (clarinets and other smaller instruments would be carried in the bus with their owner); instruments like tubas, drums, trombones and more were placed in their cases and inside a moving truck. We had to get to the school earlier than others to do this, and we would leave the game early in the fourth quarter to get all the cases ready for people to put them into to be loaded onto the truck. We did not wear our uniforms to the game—it was simply too hot—so we placed them in their garment bags and hung them from the windows until we got to the school we were playing. I remember that day our band directors stressed that we make sure and place our garment bags on the windows and keep our smaller instruments in the bus with us because they were afraid that there may be some trouble.

In truth, we knew one of the reasons we placed our bags on the windows was some high school football games fomented animosity between both sides, especially if there is already an inter-school rivalry. One dangerous result of a rivalry is that at times buses got attacked by people throwing rocks. So, the reminder from our directors seemed unusual because it was already common practice. However, we did what we were told, and all the windows had a garment bag.

We arrived at Mission High School and began to unload the bus. From the moment we set foot on the campus, you could feel an air of tension that went beyond the usual game day rivalry. As the game progressed in the first half, we could see fights breaking out in the stands and among the players. This we had not seen before, at least not on that level. Our director, Mr. Parkhill, seemed bewildered by all that was transpiring around us. Usually after performing our halftime show, we were allowed the first half of the third quarter to eat something, but that Friday night that was not the case. We had heard a rumor one of the football players' parent attempted to hit one of the referees with his car, and that was enough for Mr. Parkhill. He sought out the members of the loading crew and told us we were going to leave soon and to begin to unload the cases from the truck. We did this without question. Many of us were feeling the same fear he was, and we were more than happy to leave early.

As we were unloading the cases, we began to hear rumors there were people lining up along our route home to throw rocks at the bus, so our sense of urgency increased. Once the rest of the band joined us, we did our best to get everything loaded on the truck as fast as we could. However, there seemed to be some delay in actually leaving the school. By the time we made it out, the game was already finishing, so we waited to leave all together. The delay came from the drivers trying to find a different route back home. Right before the bus departed, we were told that those of us with instruments in the bus had to place them against the window for protection. After what seemed like a long trip—at the beginning we did hear things hitting our bus—we finally made it back to our high school. When we got off the bus, we heard that one of the D'ettes (our dance troop), Patricia Guerrero, had been struck by broken glass in her eye as an object smashed the window next to her. We unloaded the bus feeling scared and bewildered by the events of the evening. The practice of covering up the bus windows with our uniforms would take on more of a serious tone from then on.

The tension that seemed to fill the atmosphere was no doubt a product of the immense grief descending on the Mission/Alton community. Sometimes this grief manifests itself as anger at the world around you, anger at a situation you can do nothing about because it has passed and you cannot assuage the loss you have suffered. Moreover, you are no longer the person you used to be because of your loss, and you can no longer remember the

The Accident

person you were before. Sadly, in a close-knit community like Alton, it was truly a shared loss, and the community reacted to it very personally. At times, the results were not always positive. In fact, this tragic incident would tear through the very fabric of the community, affecting it to this day.

One target of the animosity within the community was Alton mayor San Juanita Zamora. On Sunday, November 19, 1989, during the early morning hours, flyers were secretly distributed to the residents of Alton. They were placed in fences and mailboxes throughout the city. Their message was directed at the mayor, making claims ranging from theft of monies donated to the victims of the accident to being a practitioner of *brujeria* (witchcraft). They were written in Spanish and were signed, "We must unmask the devil." In an interview with the local paper, *The Monitor*, Ms. Zamora was quoted as saying, "It's almost two months now, and you would think that it would be time for things to calm down. But somebody is not about to let things go."[112] The animosity toward the mayor began shortly after the accident, when questions arose about how she was handling the money donated for the victims of the bus accident. There were donations flooding in from individuals, groups and businesses, and some people in Alton began to grow suspicious as to where exactly it was all going and how it was being used?

In early October, tensions came to a head at a meeting in city hall, where there was a spirited debate on what they were going to do with the funds and the possible creation of a memorial park at the location of the accident. This idea was met with some opposition. Alton resident Mrs. Salvador Vela stated, "Who'd want their kids to play on swings near where all those kids were killed." (The park was built and is still there today; its presence is still somewhat controversial among some of the survivors.) However, the main focus of the anger and suspicion was Mayor Zamora. There were several calls from the members in attendance to have the mayor resign. One of the attendees, Oscar Cantu, described the chaos and the mayor's leadership by saying, "Instead of the city of Alton going up, it's going down. We want a new mayor."[113] The city attorney, Al Alvarez, attempted to steer the topic back to one that was immediately pressing, especially to the parents of school-age children in Alton: what was going to be done about the caliche pits.[114] This question would not be immediately resolved at the meeting.

The hostility toward the mayor revealed that not only would the accident be a tragic moment in the history of Alton, but it also had the potential to tear the community apart. The attacks on Ms. Zamora had escalated to the point that she was receiving death threats. She was told all manner of hateful and terrifying things: "How many more kids do you want to kill?" and "Come on over to the caliche pit and see how it feels."[115] Additionally, the stress of it all was taking its toll on the mayor, to the point that she sought medical attention. The antagonism did not limit itself to people demanding changes from the city government. It also spread its way into the government itself, as factions began to form for and against the mayor. This infighting became especially problematic when some members of the city council refused to attend meetings, bringing a halt to any decisions being made as to what to do about the caliche pits and how to protect the public.[116]

Sadly, the anger, animosity and jealousy reached beyond city hall. It would spill over into the community and among victims and their fellow members of the Alton community. At the center of it all was the enormous amount of money that would be awarded to victims and their families. However, that will be a later subject in this book.

THE INVESTIGATION

From the outset of the investigation, Dr Pepper truck driver Ruben Perez claimed that he attempted to stop at the stop sign, which would have prevented the accident, but his brakes did not respond.[117] This placed the blame for the accident on his employer, Valley Coca-Cola, a fact that, if proven, would be quite profitable for many a plaintiff and lawyer. Nevertheless, this argument and the criminal and civil trials would all have to await the outcome of the official investigation, conducted by the National Transportation Safety Board (NTSB). The first NTSB investigator arrived on the afternoon of the day of the accident, and after the District Attorney's Office obtained a search warrant for the Dr Pepper truck, the investigation began.[118] The ten-person NTSB investigative team stated that the examination would consist of ten days in the field, but its report would not be issued for a year.[119]

The NTSB team's initial visual inspection of the Dr Pepper truck's braking system revealed no obvious faults; however, further mechanical testing would also have to be conducted. That Sunday, September 24, the NTSB conducted field tests with the Dr Pepper trailer that caused the accident. They attached the trailer to a truck similar to the one being driven by Ruben Perez at the time of the accident and utilized only the brakes of the original trailer. The team found that the brakes were sufficient enough to bring the vehicle to a stop. It was driven at speeds ranging from twenty to thirty miles per hour, and the truck was able to stop every time. Nevertheless, the vehicle

The Accident

The Monitor newspaper front-page article on the beginning of the NTSB investigation and the loss of Ysenia Perez, fifteen, who succumbed to her injuries in the hospital. *From* The Monitor, *September 22, 1989.*

The Alton Bus Crash

Above: *Progress Times* photo of the bus lying on its back outside the pit. *From the* Progress Times, *September 27, 1989.*

Left: *Progress Times* photo of the Dr Pepper truck after the collision. *From the* Progress Times, *September 27, 1989.*

loader, Ruben Pena, as quoted by NTSB chief Bob Bartlett, stated, "The driver applied the foot brake, trailer brake and downshifted" all within three hundred feet of the intersection.[120] These actions should have been sufficient to have stopped the truck.

Further examinations conducted by the NTSB revealed other faults within the vehicle itself. To begin with, it was discovered that out of the six brakes the Dr Pepper truck possessed, three of them had not been adjusted properly. Next, the team members found a crack in the diaphragm of an air hose that was also part of the braking system.[121] NTSB member Lee Dickinson pointed out that "under Federal Department of Transportation regulations, had an inspection been conducted on this truck prior to its departure, it would have been pulled out of service."[122] This finding would go on to help in Ruben Perez's defense.

However, as Robert Floyd, president of Texas Motor Transportation Association, pointed out, the regulations Dickinson was alluding to had their implementation delayed within the state of Texas.[123] The president laid the

The Accident

blame for this delay squarely at the feet of "wholesale beer and soft drink distributors," along with legislators and lobbyists who had pushed back the date for the implementation of the new safety standards to October 1 (nine days after the accident) from its initial January 1998 date.[124] One of the people responsible for the delay, Representative Mark Stiles (D), who owned a concrete company, explained, "We want safety.…There was no concern over the cost of safety. The problem is you can't have an inspection of every truck every day by some public personnel. The company has to be responsible. The driver has to be responsible."[125] The shifting of the responsibility to the driver and not an inspector or the company was one way to shift the financial liability to an individual and not a company or the government, each of which has much deeper pockets than a truck driver. Nonetheless, Dickinson pointed out that the NTSB "wasn't ready to pinpoint the brakes or any other factor as the cause of the Sep. 21 accident near Alton."[126]

As much as people were waiting on the NTSB to lay the blame on a particular individual or company, the NTSB had pointed out from the beginning that it was not only there to determine the cause of the accident but also to protect the public's future safety and make recommendations to prevent further accidents.[127] In the end, the NTSB would state in its report:

> [T]*he probable cause of the accident was the truck driver's inattention and subsequent failure to maintain sufficient control of his vehicle to stop at the stop sign. Contributing to the severity of the accident was the lack of a sufficient number of emergency exits on the school bus to accommodate the rapid egress of all 81 students.*[128]

The board would go on to recommend that a review should be made of the adequacy of the number of exits on a school bus; how federal, state and local officials respond to mass casualty accidents; training of emergency personnel; school bus driver training; review of vehicle maintenance by Valley Coca-Cola; driver training for Valley Coca-Cola; and crashworthiness of school buses.[129] NTSB's finding was that, like in most accidents, the loss of life is hardly ever attributable to one specific thing; it is usually a conglomeration of factors that line themselves up in such a way as to create an environment for a large loss of life. The "driver's inattention was just the first in this tragic combination of events." As a result, the NTSB's report could be seen by both the prosecution and the defense as helpful at trial. It did mention the drivers, but it went on to mention other factors, such as lack of exits, and its recommendations also allude to the fact that the response by authorities could have been handled better. Thus, with the NTSB's study concluded, the ball was now in the court of Hidalgo County district attorney Rene Guerra.

On Tuesday, November 21, 1989, Ruben Perez was officially indicted with twenty-one counts of involuntary manslaughter for the September 21 accident. In the state of Texas, manslaughter is considered a third-degree felony, and its punishment is a maximum prison sentence of up to ten years in prison, along with a $10,000 fine. Perez pleaded not guilty to all charges and was released on $75,000 bond. Along with the indictment, the grand jury handed a letter to the judge asking for the NTSB to conduct further inquiries into the accident.[130] Two members of the NTSB, Jim Burnett and Lee Dickinson, had asked for a public inquiry to be conducted over the matter because the original recommendation had been to close the case without a public inquiry, and they were advocating for a change in the NTSB decision. Burnett and Dickinson felt that a public investigation would serve the public in highlighting the issue of school bus safety. However, there were some on the board who were content with the investigation being closed.

One such individual was District Attorney Rene Guerra. Guerra stated that a further investigation "would possibly interfere with the prosecution" of Perez.[131] Nevertheless, the board denied the request due to "lack of resources and the absence of national impact on safety issues," a decision from which both Burnett and Dickinson dissented.[132] In the end, the accident and changes that were enacted as a direct result of this tragic accident would have a national impact on school bus manufacturing and safety to this day.

Public reactions to the NTSB's final report ran along similar lines. Justino Regalado, a father whose two daughters died as a result of the accident, stated that neither he nor anyone else should continue to maintain any hatred toward anyone: "It could have happened to anyone." Fidel Lopez, who harbored a considerable amount of animosity toward the driver who had taken his daughter, stated that when it came to blame and a trial, "What do I gain from him going to prison if it's not going to bring back our daughter?" Carmen Cruz lost one of her daughters in the accident. Her reaction was that, in the end, she would trust the courts to decide and added, "There has been a lot of suffering from the accident, and I'm sure Ruben has suffered too, but not nearly as much as the families who lost loved ones."[133] The similarity of the responses and the lack of feelings of vengeance toward the man whom the NTSB now blamed for the deaths of their children highlight what was at the forefront of these parents' minds: their children. They saw that anything less than bringing their children back was not worth their attention. The loss of a child is something that any parent would give their life to prevent. As Ms. Cruz pointed out, when it came to what was going to happen to Ruben Perez, it would be up to the local courts to decide, and District Attorney Rene Guerra would do his best to provide the community with some sort of justice.

PART II
THE COURTS

THE CRIMINAL TRIAL OF RUBEN PEREZ: THE PROSECUTION

Hidalgo County district attorney Rene Guerra heard about the accident as he entered the courthouse after his routine cup of coffee at the Echo Hotel in Edinburg, Texas, which is just down the road from the courthouse. His initial reaction was one of shock while he digested all the details given to him. Mr. Guerra then went into district attorney mode. Being the Hidalgo County DA and prosecutor for decades, he knew his responsibility was to the public. An accident of that nature and magnitude would more than likely result in a criminal trial, and he was already thinking that this case would fit the charge of negligent homicide if not involuntary manslaughter. Mr. Guerra stated when interviewed in the summer of 2018, "From a prosecutor's perspective, when you hear about multiple deaths in traffic, somebody's at fault."

As District Attorney Guerra learned more details about the accident, he decided to finalize the charge at involuntary manslaughter: "This was back in '89 and there were no cellphones. All you had for a distraction was your passenger, the radio, or you falling asleep, so there was nothing that would have impacted the driver's perception. The driver said he did not see the sign coming up, but his loader said he tried to warn him about the stop sign. It was his subsequent faulty reaction that led to the deaths." Mr. Guerra went on to add, "Someone who runs a stop sign and kills 21 kids ruins a lot of

Jury selection begins in Alton bus crash trial

By PANFILO GARCIA
The Monitor

EDINBURG — Prosecutors and defense attorneys on Tuesday pared down to 120 the number of potential jurors for the highly-publicized involuntary manslaughter trial of Ruben Perez.

Perez, 28, stands trial on 21 involuntary manslaughter counts in connection with the Sept. 21, 1989, Alton school bus accident at Bryan Road and Five Mile Line.

■ Rejected Jurors Speak — 2A

Perez was driving a soft drink delivery truck when it collided with the bus filled with children. The bus was sent careening into a water-filled caliche pit.

More than 80 potential jurors were released Monday for various reasons, including that some had already formed an opinion about Perez' guilt or innocence.

One juror began crying as she told the judge that she went to school with some of the victims in the collision.

"It was an accident — there shouldn't have been a charge," another disqualified jurist said. And a third told the judge, "the defendant was guilty since the first time I heard this."

During Jury Selection: Ruben Perez, center, sits with defense attorney Bob Binder, left, and lead attorney Joseph Connors in the first day of jury selection for Perez's trial involving the Sept. 21, 1989 Alton school bus accident.
Ric Vasquez / The Monitor

The remaining potential jurors were given a questionnaire concerning the amount of publicity they had witnessed about the incident.

"There has been a lot of publicity about this suit," State District Judge Fidencio Guerra told jurors. "What you see on TV is not necessarily the truth.

"(Perez) comes in innocent," Guerra said. "The basic question is going to be, 'can the state prove what they say happened?'"

Earlier Tuesday, Hidalgo County District Attorney Rene Guerra complained that defense attorney Joseph Connors added about 90 names to his list of potential defense witnesses Monday.

"I think that's an abuse of subpoena powers," Guerra, not related to the judge, said at a pretrial hearing. "A lot of the subpoenas have nothing to do with the case."

Connors answered, "Mr. Guerra should have dismissed this case a"

See **TRIAL** page 2A

The Monitor newspaper headline. *From* The Monitor, *April 14, 1993.*

families, but you look at it, and you want to feel sorry for this guy. But he decided to take on the responsibility to be a professional truck driver, and I think he had the experience to operate the vehicle safely. He did not set out to cause this accident, but he was not paying proper attention. His reaction was faulty and with the heavy load he was carrying, since he had only made one stop, the accident happened."[134]

The fact that Ruben Perez stated he did not see the sign and his loader had to warn him does not fully match the NTSB's findings, which stated that Mr. Perez was on his usual route. As pointed out earlier, Mr. Perez refused to be interviewed by the NTSB. The investigators did have the full cooperation of Valley Coca-Cola, and the company stated that he had been on that route since August, so he should have been familiar with it, including where the stop signs are. These remain troubling questions to this day because of the acquittal and Mr. Perez's continued silence. Ruben was approached about an interview but refused to add any more to the story. Consequently, an examination of that day's events will never be a complete affair; lacking his side of the story, one has only the evidence, the investigative report and other eyewitnesses.

Mr. Guerra brought the evidence before a grand jury, which handed down a twenty-one-count sealed indictment two months after the accident

Artist Estrella Garcia's depiction of the arrest of Ruben Perez. *Courtesy of the artist.*

occurred. As part of the deliberations, the jury was given both the NTSB report and a report issued by the Texas Department of Public Safety. The jurors also received the coroner's report placing the cause of death for the children as drowning and not from injuries sustained in the crash.[135] The coroner's report would actually assist in the civil litigation against Blue Bird Bus Company (the manufacturer of the bus)—the crash was indeed survivable had the children been able to make it out of the bus and out of the water in which they drowned.

The jury foreman, Ms. Olivia Hernandez, commented on the proceedings, saying, "It was a difficult decision."[136] Mr. Guerra agreed, responding, "I don't think any grand jury in these United States faced with the same situation would not have had a difficult decision."[137] Along with the handing down of the indictment, the jury felt it pertinent to send a letter to the presiding judge, Fernando Mancias, to ask him to ask the NTSB to do further research on school bus safety.[138] The NTSB included in its report a list of recommendations that resulted from its findings, but it would not conduct further research into school safety. In the end, that would be done by others.

The charges remained sealed until the arrest of Mr. Ruben Perez, who at the time of the grand jury's decision was seeking psychiatric care in Corpus Christi, Texas. Corpus Christi was probably chosen as it was a more than two-hour drive from the Valley and hence far enough away from Alton to not be confronted by angry residents. Nonetheless, he turned himself in later that day.[139]

The criminal case was heard in the 370th District Court and presided over by a unique personality in the Texas judicial circuit, Judge Fidencio Guerra (no relation to Rene Guerra). In a February 2006 *Texas Observer* article, "The Worst Judges in Texas: In These Courtrooms Justice Comes to a Screeching Halt," reporter Nate Blakeslee sought to find out who were the "bad judges" of Texas. He described his methodology:

> *We began our search with no preconceived notion as to what makes a judge "bad." Instead we talked to dozens of attorneys, including former*

prosecutors and judges, to find out what makes them mutter around the water cooler. We heard stories—virtually all off the record, for obvious reasons—about incompetent judges, partisan judges, insane judges, mean judges, and judges on a mission that had little to do with justice.[140]

At the end of this process, Mr. Fidencio Guerra ranked fifth on the list of worst judges in Texas. The article cited his use of sock puppets in court and a case of domestic abuse in which he made the offending husband hold his wife's hand and apologize to her. He then denied the woman's request for a protective order, reasoning that if he beats her, she can file charges of assault, and if he murders her, he can be indicted for murder.[141]

When it came to the trial of Ruben Perez, Judge Fidencio Guerra made what seemed like a strange requirement of the media that was covering the case. He asked that every time the case was reported on, journalists must include his name and the court's name. News director for local ABC News Affiliate Rick Diaz stated, "In 25 years in television, I've never had this happen. I find this very unusual....Most judges prefer that the media cover their cases, so, barring somebody from the court—I don't know what he wants to accomplish with that."[142] He was referring to threats to bar those who didn't comply with the judge's orders and restrictions as to what to shoot in his courtroom.[143]

The reaction from fellow news director of the local CBS affiliate KGBT-TV Jeff Koch was along the same lines as Diaz, explaining, "My immediate reaction was why? I don't mind guidelines of a case that's of a sensitive nature, like this one. But when he just wants to see his name in print or on the television, then I don't know what purpose that could possibly serve."[144] In his defense, Judge Guerra responded that having his name in the media spotlight would be a means of holding him accountable for his decisions on the bench, stating, "By knowing the judge, they'll know what judge to blame if they think the judge is working or isn't working."[145] One argument for the need for publicity is the fact that eventually Fidencio Guerra would need to run for reelection, and name recognition does go a long way toward results at the polling booth. But it does, as the judge pointed out, highlight to the public who is making the decisions on such crucial cases such as that of the Alton Bus Crash.

Ruben Perez's courtroom struggles began even before the actual trial started. In the jury selection process, Perez's legal counsel, Joseph Connors, and 370th District judge Fidencio Guerra Jr. clashed over a questionnaire that Connors wanted potential jurors to fill out. Many of the questions had to do with the amount of knowledge potential jurors had about the accident and their opinions. Guerra grew annoyed with Connors, at one point suggesting moving the trial to Nome, Alaska. Moving the trial was one of more than one hundred pretrial motions Connors filed on behalf of his client. In the end, after striking some of the questions, Judge Guerra approved the questionnaire.[146]

The question of publicity was a fair one. Since the day of the accident, the story was being covered nationally throughout the United States and internationally to nearby Mexico. For many of those touched by the accident, Mexico was held close to their hearts and a place where many of them had relatives and extended families. In a sense, this was a binational story tearing at heartstrings on both sides of the border. On the American side, the story was covered by the national news organizations like ABC, NBC and CBS. The incident was even the subject of a long-form ABC news show called *Day One*. Therefore, the possibility that the jury pool would already have some perceived notions about guilt or innocence was a very real question and could impede a fair and impartial trial.

One of the other flashpoints between Connors and DA Guerra involved the sheer number of witnesses that Connors was submitting for the judge's approval, making the number of defense witnesses more than one hundred.[147] DA Guerra noted, "I think that's an abuse of subpoena power....A lot of the subpoenas have nothing to do with the case."[148] Connors retorted, "Mr. Guerra should have dismissed this case a long time ago. He's the one that is causing this to go to trial."[149] This exchange and the constant legal wrangling were signs of things to come on just how contentious Ruben Perez's criminal trial would be.

In the end, the pool of two hundred potential jurors was whittled down to fourteen, or twelve plus two alternates. It consisted of mostly female jurors, as only two men would serve on the jury. The process was long, taking more than three days, and was prolonged by the contentious questionnaire created by Connors and the fact that the lawyers ended up questioning fifty potential jurors on an individual basis. The main factor in dismissal of jurors was publicity and personal bias. One potential juror broke down because she knew one of the victims of the accident. One reason for some of the men to be stricken from the jury was their expertise in automotive knowledge.[150] The dismissal of individuals with such knowledge was perhaps due to the fact that they might have reason not to accept some of the defense witnesses' testimony. In a sense, this might weaken the strength of the defense's strategy and their confidence in it.

In a nod toward the seriousness and impact of Ruben Perez's trial, District Attorney Rene Guerra decided to prosecute the case himself.[151] The case District Attorney Guerra presented to the jury would be one in keeping with what he had learned from the NTSB and DPS reports on the accident. He pointed out to the jury that the tests done on the truck's brakes revealed that they were able to stop the truck in time to avoid the fatal collision. This was contrary to Mr. Perez's claim that the brakes were not working. Additionally, he also sought to counter the claim that Ruben made about not being able to see the stop sign at the intersection where the accident happened by explaining to the jury that this was Mr. Perez's assigned route, so he had to be familiar with it. He also brought Ruben Pena to testify that he was the loader and sitting in the passenger seat. He testified that Mr. Perez was driving at forty-five miles per hour when he noticed he was not slowing down, causing him to warn him of the upcoming stop.[152]

At this point, there were two apparent contradictions to the defendant's claims. One, that the route was unknown to Ruben Perez, and second, that he was speeding. According to the NTSB report, the last posted speed limit was thirty miles per hour. This argument could be bolstered by the fact that, as was also revealed in the NTSB report, Mr. Perez had been involved in an accident before, for which his license had been taken away, and he had barely been able to have it reinstated before being allowed back on as a driver.[153] Moving back to the first point, the fact that the loader Mr. Pena either knew of or could see the sign coming up—because he warned Ruben of its upcoming presence—presents a refutation of Mr. Perez's claims. If the loader knew the route and the presence of the stop sign or could see it, then Ruben had to have knowledge of or see it as well.

DA Guerra's case was not just attacked by the defense; his whole character and motivation were challenged by lead defense attorney Joseph Connors. Mr. Connors accused the prosecution of being steered and motivated by attorneys from Valley Coca-Cola. Rene Guerra shot back, angrily declaring Mr. Connors's statement as a "damnable lie!" Attorney Joe E. Garcia, one of the lawyers representing Coca-Cola, called the allegations "libelous and slanderous."[154] No doubt Mr. Garcia's statement on Connors's claims did fit the definitions of libel and slander, but these accusations were all part of the defense's strategy to shift the blame away from the accused. In fact, when survivor Sandra Garcia testified about the difficulties trying to escape from the bus, Connors began to include the Blue Bird Bus Company as another party that was at fault. The district attorney attempted to redirect the argument back to the defense. DA

Guerra counterclaimed that the defense was only attempting to draw more media attention, as this would help in an upcoming civil suit of Ruben Perez versus Valley Coca-Cola, pointing out to the courtroom, "We are not advocating for anyone else's case in this courtroom....It's a shock to me that the system is being used in this way." Connors responded that he "was in no position to obtain fees from Perez's civil lawsuit."

THE CRIMINAL TRIAL OF RUBEN PEREZ: THE DEFENSE

The prosecution rested after presenting its case for four days, and the damage the defense was able to inflict became clear when at the end of the four days, presiding judge Fidencio Guerra decided to reduce the charges from involuntary manslaughter to criminally negligent homicide. The prosecution realized that its case was not as convincing as it thought it was, but Rene Guerra went on to argue the fact: "There is no evidence that would give rise to a total brake failure, as the defense would have everybody believe.... If there's no evidence, then I haven't been present in the courtroom these past four days, and it's been a waste of the state's time."[155] However, what apparently the judge had seen throughout the prosecution's testimony was the effectiveness of the defense's attacks. Connors grilled Texas Department of Public Safety accident investigator Francisco Elizondo for more than eight hours, spending a great amount of time on questions of the physics of the accident. Connors spent so much time on this issue that Rene Guerra responded, "These calculations are hard to follow unless you're a math major or wizard."[156]

Additionally, Connors pointed out that many of the prosecution's witnesses were actually helping the defense instead of strengthening the prosecution's case. Arturo Garza, one of Perez's supervisors, painted a sympathetic image of Ruben Perez, describing how distraught he was in the ambulance as he rode away from the accident site, hoping that none of the children was hurt in the accident.[157] Connors told the jury that all the testimony given by Perez's employers revealed him to be a good employee, as Garza described him: "He was very excited about his job. His dream was to drive the biggest trailer that the company had." Also, forensic pathologist Ruben Santos (a witness for the prosecution) placed the cause of death of all twenty-one students as drowning, stating, "This was not a killing accident." This played into the defense's hand because it gave the team someone else to lay the blame on, the City of Alton, for not placing barriers for the public safety.[158] Connors did not cross-examine all the witnesses the prosecution put on the stand because "he planned to unleash a surprise attack once Guerra had revealed his strategy."[159] Connors stated, "If Mr. Guerra can't prove it on his own, why should I help?...I can just keep my mouth shut and Mr. Guerra can either prove it or not prove it."[160]

Connors began his defense with a dramatic description of the accident and the truck that Ruben was driving, which he described as "a loaded missile that Coca Cola sent out day after day...exploded at the intersection of Bryan road and 5 mile line....Coca Cola messed up and not my client."[161] The comparing of the truck to a loaded missile was clearly a reference to the argument Connors was planning to use later in the trial about Coca-Cola's lack of training and truck inspections. This would shift the blame to the company. Painting a picture of a company that was acting in complete disregard for the public's safety planted the seed of the typical evil corporate entity whose only goal was that of profits, obtained over the lives of these students.

At the center of Perez's defense lay several crucial points, most of which had been highlighted in the NTSB report. First, he was a victim of Valley Coca-Cola's cutbacks in the area of maintenance and in his training.[162] Perez had only attended ten hours of "behind-the-wheel instruction from other drivers."[163] His only real instruction came from his time driving with his father.

Another point brought up in the trial was the fact that if the pit had been surrounded by a proper barrier, there would have been little or no loss of life as a result of the collision.[164] After all, the earliest industry in Alton, before it was even incorporated into a city, was the excavation and sale of caliche for building projects. In all the decades of having open caliche pits, something should have been done to protect the safety of motorists from falling into one. Besides, there had already been an accident with loss of life in one of these open pits. This argument was coupled with the fact that the coroner had already testified that the crash was survivable if they had not landed into a (man-made) body of water.

Using photos, Connors described how branches from trees obstructed Perez's view of the stop sign.[165] This was an attempt to corroborate Ruben Perez's account that he did not see the stop sign and was not aware he was coming up to a stop sign and intersection until he was warned by his loader, Mr. Pena. At that point, he did his best to stop the vehicle.

In keeping with the defense's strategy of shifting the blame away from Ruben Perez, Robert Reed testified on behalf of Blue Bird Company (the bus's manufacturer). Blue Bird had paid out $23 million in settlements to the victims and the families of those involved in the accident.[166] To the defense, this was proof in keeping with the coroner's testimony that the accident was survivable if the students had only been able to exit the bus. The deaths, then, occurred from the lack of barrier around the caliche pit and the inability of the students to exit from the bus due to lack of easy exits provided by the bus's manufacturer.

The final witness for the defense, Dan Asa (who had been hired by the Texas Department of Public Safety to inspect the brakes), would be used to corroborate Ruben Perez's account of how the accident transpired. Mr. Asa pointed out that the evidence showed that Valley Coca-Cola had not been in compliance with the truck manufacturer's five-year maintenance schedule. This schedule called for an inspection every two thousand miles, which should have headed off any potential damage or accidents long before the truck's maintenance or lack thereof could create such a dangerous situation. In fact, documentation showed that it had been more than four thousand miles since the truck had been inspected. Additionally, Dan Asa found contamination within the brake lines themselves. They were able to draw out two quarts of oily sludge from inside the air tank that connected to the truck's braking system. All of these details would have been easily discovered during what should have been a routine inspection of the braking system and the truck as a whole.[167] The condition the brakes were in would have caused them to behave erratically, working one day and not working the next. "That's why you keep contaminants out of the system," Mr. Asa remarked to the court.[168]

Mr. Asa would also go on to corroborate Mr. Perez's testimony as to his actions when he became aware of the upcoming stop sign and the possible collision with the school bus testifying, "My opinion is that the driver attempted to downshift with the ordinary standards of care that most drivers would....It was Coca Cola that was responsible. They were responsible for the truck and the driver."[169] District Attorney Rene Guerra did his best to send numerous objections to the questions being leveled at Dan Asa by defense co-counsel Bob Binder, only to have them overruled by Judge Fidencio Guerra. In attempt to save his case, Mr. Guerra asked Mr. Asa if he would at least reconsider the "F" grade he had assigned to Coca-Cola's maintenance practices, to which he responded that he would modify it to an "F-."

Finally, Mr. Asa pointed to tests that had been run on trucks whose brakes were properly maintained and a truck with brakes that were in similar in condition to the Dr Pepper truck that Mr. Perez was driving on the day of the accident. Both trucks were placed in similar conditions as those on that day. They were both traveling at forty-five miles per hour, and they had three hundred feet before they hit the intersection. In the truck with properly maintained brakes, the truck was able to stop in time. However, the second truck failed to stop on time, every time.[170] This was the defense's proof that it was most certainly Coca-Cola's maintenance practices that caused the accident and not Ruben, who did everything he was supposed to do to stop from hitting the bus. This was in direct contradiction to similar tests done by the NTSB to determine if the brakes were inadequate, but in its findings, the truck was able to stop in time. In the end, Connors did everything in his power to establish a case for reasonable doubt. If one or all of these details were true, then Perez was not solely responsible for the accident.

At the end of the testimony, the jury was faced with two very different explanations as to what happened on that fateful day. The prosecution attempted to show to the jury what it believed were basic facts about the case using the evidence provided by the NTSB, the Texas Department of Public Safety and the testimony of eyewitnesses and experts. The picture it attempted to paint for the jury was that Ruben Perez knew the route he was on and should have known that there was a stop and intersection coming up. It was his lack of attention that caused him to react too slow, and had he been a more attentive driver, he could have been able to prevent the tragedy. After all, he was the only person behind the wheel of the Dr Pepper truck; had he not hit the bus, there would have been no injuries or deaths. In short, the fact the pit was open and it was difficult to get out of the bus played no role in the fact that none of that would have mattered had he been a better driver.

The defense painted a very different picture for the jury. In its version of the events, Ruben Perez was very much one of the victims of this horrible tragedy. Ruben was a sympathetic figure who unluckily was put at the helm of a "loaded missile" instead of a simple delivery truck. He tried his best to stop the truck on an unfamiliar road, but unfortunately for him, Valley Coca-Cola's lax maintenance practice had allowed the brakes on Perez's truck to fall well below safe standards. This accident was made even more tragic because Valley Coca-Cola was not the only culprit. The company had two accomplices in the City of Alton and Blue Bird Bus Company. If the city had addressed the ongoing issue of open caliche pits in the city long before September 21, 1989, there would have been no open pit for the out-of-control bus to fall into. Finally, if Blue Bird had manufactured a bus with a view toward safety and multiple points of egress, the children would have been able to escape from the water-filled bus.

Consequently, as the coroner report stated, it was a survivable accident, but the reason these students met their end was the neglect of the city and faulty manufacturing. After the jury was excused, the defense attempted to get all the charges dropped but was denied, and the case was sent to the jury.[171] The defense reasoned that it had made a clear case and was even able to use prosecution witness to support its theory on what really happened that day.

On Thursday May 6, 1993, Ruben Perez's criminal case came to an end with an acquittal. On his way out of the courtroom, a very distraught-looking and almost broken young man was swarmed by reporters, camera lights and microphones. He responded to years of name calling by stating in a low voice, "I'm no killer, I'm no drug addict or alcoholic. A lot of people blame me of that, it hurts."[172] Most assuredly this young man had been through quite an ordeal. Even though some of the victims' parents did not harbor any ill will toward him, he was the focus of a great deal of hatred and threats. These threats grew to a point that Valley Coca-Cola had to hire an armed guard to watch over him at his home. This was on top of Ruben having the deaths of twenty-one young children weighing on his conscience, so much so that shortly before the trial, he was briefly institutionalized. His sister, who was a nurse at McAllen Medical Center (one of the hospitals which some of the victims of the accident were taken to), had to quit her job to take of her brother full time.[173] Like all those involved in the accident, he would forever bear the emotional scars of what happened that day by the pit.

Meanwhile, his elated defense team looked on to its impending suit against his former employer, Valley Coca-Cola, stating, "Obviously a not guilty verdict is going to assist us in the civil case."[174] Without a doubt, Ruben Perez's case, with the backing of an acquittal, would be added to the growing tally of lawsuits that had sprung up from the accident. His acquittal would shift the blame to the two targets of the defense's attacks. Because the accident did happen, and if the courts said that Ruben Perez was not to blame, then someone else was—someone with much deeper pockets than a young truck driver. The jury's decision went on to affect the civil proceedings that were already making their way through the courts.

To litigators, Ruben's acquittal meant that the burden on Valley Coca-Cola and Blue Bird Bus Company to defend themselves from lawsuits was markedly heavier than it once was, and their need for a quick settlement grew even more. The next phase of this story would play itself out in civil courts and the law offices of local and out-of-town lawyers. Sadly, it would be in the pursuit of finding someone to blame and providing some sort of closure to those left behind that these families would fall victim once again—victim to greed, unethical behavior and unscrupulous business tactics. They would also be exposed to jealousy from people inside their community, and finally, for others avarice would provoke questionable actions. In the end, between the criminal trial and the lawsuits, the community of Alton would never be the same.

THE LAWSUITS

On June 27, 2010, an article titled "Bitter Divorce Reveals Unflattering Side of South Texas Legal System" was printed in *The Monitor* and contained within it is a glaring example of the amount of money that was made by those involved in the civil litigation of the Alton Bus Crash. However, these people were not victims or families of the victims; some were "facilitators" and lawyers. The article described the home of one such "facilitator":

> *A wheeler-dealer of the first rate, the 47-year-old former emergency medical technician had amassed a $30 million fortune in just under two decades. His 8,500-square-foot home in Mission featured a private gym, a movie theater and a fine art collection that included works by Salvador Dali and Pablo Picasso. And he helmed a business that brought in $1.5 million a month from its involvement in the world's most lucrative personal injury cases.*[175]

One of these "lucrative personal injury cases" was the Alton Bus Crash. The subject of this article is Wilfredo "Willie" Garcia, who at the time of the accident was not a lawyer. He was, as the article stated, an emergency medical technician, or EMT. It was in this capacity that Garcia, after retrieving the dead, referred the parents of the deceased to law firms for which he received payment, known as "case running." This method helped many a "facilitator," and the lawyers who employ them, earn large amounts of money in the process.[176]

'Unethical' attorneys are said trying to move in on families

By JACKIE LARSON

While volunteers have moved in to help victims and survivors of last week's Mission school bus accident, some members of the legal profession are moving in for business.

"Unethical" attorneys, some from upstate, are still moving in on victims families, according to one Houston lawyer.

The Monitor has received reports of at least two families being approached to sign papers. The mother of one victim was approached by an attorney at a funeral home during visitation. "It's not the place to do business" an upset friend reported.

A counselor attending to a family told The Monitor an attorney had come to the home of the victim's parents, knocked on the door and approached the family with papers. "But they are naive.

See LAWYERS page 2A

The Monitor newspaper headline about the lawsuits connected to the accident. *From* The Monitor, *September 25, 1989.*

The Alton bus accident would be referred to as the "one of the biggest personal injury free-for-alls the Valley had ever seen."[177] Indeed, much like sharks attracted to blood, lawyers were attracted to Coca-Cola's deep pockets. From day one of the accident, lawyers from as far away as Dallas and Houston made their way to the small town of Alton. Many lawyers, like the dedicated school officials and Red Cross counselors, traveled door to door throughout the community. Dora Rodriguez, the mother of one of the victims, managed to collect a three-inch-high stack of business cards from lawyers and their "case runners" who solicited her for their business.[178] Another word for "case running" is *barratry*, which is against the law. Barratry brings with it a $2,000 fine, and multiple convictions can be bumped up to a felony. However, an even more serious consequence was that it could lead to disbarment. The numerous reports of barratry that emerged from the Alton Bus Crash resulted in the American Bar Association having to send a "disaster team" to the area to investigate the growing number of allegations.[179] In fact, President Darrell Jordan of the Texas State Bar stated that the events in Alton "dissapoin[t] me greatly."[180]

However, it was not just the solicitation of the clients that the American Bar Association and local authorities found surprising; it was also the manner in which they were successfully able to sign a client to them. In order to get a family member to sign "on the dotted line," lawyers engaged in trickery, offering of financial incentives and flat-out intimidation. Carmen Cruz stated that she had been approached by at least half a

Law firm charges bus accident clients were lured away

By REY GUEVARA V.

EDINBURG — A San Antonio lawyer called a McAllen law firm "a bunch of crybabies" after he and his partner were sued for allegedly stealing away an Alton tragedy client.

"I think it's a joke," said Jim Perkins of the suit filed by the law firm of Flores, Munoz, Hockema & Reed.

"Some lawyers are spoilsports," Perkins added. "They don't have a suit. It's nothing more than harrassment. I told them that when they called me whining about it. It's ludicruous, ridiculous and irresponsible for these so-called Valley lawyers to be filing such a b.s. lawsuit."

The suit alleges that Perkins and attorney Ruben Sandoval induced the Juan Fidel and Ismelda Lopez family to break their contract with the McAllen lawyers.

The Lopez family is one of several Alton families suing Coca Cola Bottling Co. as a result of the Alton bus crash in which 21 schoolchildren, including their daughter, Ruby, died.

Roger Reed, a partner with the suing law firm, accused Perkins and Sandoval of greedy tactics and filed for a temporary injunction Thursday against the San Antonio lawyers to stop them from communicating with the Lopez family and, ultimately, get them off the Lopez case.

"Such avaricious, selfish tactics by the defendants not only have again victimized

See BUS, Page 12A

The Monitor newspaper headline about the Flores family's legal troubles. *From* The Monitor, *September 17, 1989.*

dozen lawyers who promised money, a new car and even a new home if she signed with them.[181] In another instance, it was found that some lawyers were approaching families and having them sign contracts written in English, even though all they spoke was Spanish. This allowed for attorneys to be able to charge a rate of 45 percent instead of the typical 35 percent that lawyers collect in cases such as those in Alton, where they took no payments up front.[182] On the other hand, there was one case of intimidation that stands out beyond all the others.

The parents of survivor Nora Manriquez, age twelve, had to ask the court for a restraining order against San Antonio–based attorney Roberto Guerra in order to keep the lawyer from contacting the family. The Manriquezes had initially retained the services of Guerra as their attorney in the pending litigation against Valley Coca-Cola. However, they subsequently released him from their service and retained another attorney. Nevertheless, the family claimed that he frequently attempted to contact them and even offered them $700 to rehire him. The Manriquezes then claimed that he threatened to have another attorney assigned specifically to Nora to ensure that her best interests were being looked out for, which would cut the family out of any decisions in regards to the lawsuit.[183]

ALEX'S STORY

Alex De Leon's experience with settlements truly highlights the practices and the mindset of the time. He was in his home when his cousin knocked at his front door. As he opened it, his cousin asked if he had gotten a lawyer yet. Alex knew that his mother wanted one lawyer for the whole family since both he and his sister were involved in the accident, but he was eighteen, young and wanted to set out on his own. He saw retaining his own lawyer and getting a settlement just for himself as the means to his young selfish ends. He asked his cousin if the lawyer would be willing to give him an advance. His cousin ran back to the truck that had brought him to the house and came back to let him know that they would talk over the advance at the lawyer's home—but he would get one. He arranged for them to pick him up that evening.[184]

The man he was dealing with was Felipe Garcia, who worked out of Ramon Garcia's office, and it was at Felipe's house where they met and discussed his contract and advance. First he asked Alex if he was okay with the lawyer taking 40 percent of any settlement he would get from Coca-Cola, and Alex agreed he would accept that. He was then told that if he signed the contract, he would receive a $10,000 advance on his future settlement. Alex then explained to Mr. Garcia that if he signed the contract, his stepfather and mother would be very angry with him, and he would have to move out of the house. Felipe offered to help him get an apartment and buy him a car. This was exactly what an eighteen-year-old rebellious young man was looking for, so he went ahead and signed the contract. Later that same week, he was taken to the bank, and a check for $10,000 was deposited into his account. He was also set up in an apartment and given a 1981 Toyota Corolla that Felipe's brother, a bail bondsman, had acquired from one of his clients. Alex would later say about his actions:

> *It really put a dent in my relationship because I was being greedy and selfish. I did not realize at the time that it was going to change my life forever. It was almost as if I had abandoned my family, but when you are young and they are waving money in your face, being that young I thought it was a fortune. But it did pull me away from my family. I don't blame anyone else for my actions. I take responsibility for the decisions I made and I am still living with the consequences.*[185]

Indeed, this would create a rift in the family that would take years to heal. Today, Alex and his mother have grown very close, but there was a long period of time when he was estranged from his family. Thankfully, they are now back together and reestablishing their bonds.

LULAC

One incident that represents a microcosm of what was happening regarding the issue of lawsuits, lawyers and animosity associated with the Alton Bus Crash is what occurred within the oldest Latin American civil rights organization, the League of United Latin American Citizens (LULAC). LULAC was founded in 1929 and traces the roots of its founding to the end of the Mexican-American War, after which many Mexicans found themselves living in the United States because the border had shifted. As a result of the war, America gained what is now the Southwest. As part of this incorporation into the United States, Mexican Americans began to face racial prejudices and denial of civil rights. The most severe area was the state of Texas.

Three individual groups had been formed to combat the prejudices the Mexican American community was facing: the Order of the Sons of America, which had branches in Somerset, Corpus Christi, Peasall and San Antonio; the Knights of America in San Antonio; and the League of Latin American Citizens, with branches in Harlingen, Brownsville, Laredo, Penitas, La Grulla, McAllen and Gulf. After a two-year effort by Ben Garza, leader of Council no. 4 of the Order of the Sons of America in Corpus Christi, the three organizations merged under the name of LULAC.[186] The civil rights organization would go on to challenge segregation policies in court and defend the rights of the Mexican American community, but when it came to the Alton Bus Crash, it would certainly not live up to its founding principles. Like many others, it became mired in greed, infighting and mistrust.

On October 9, 1989, then national president of LULAC Jose De Lara penned a letter to LULAC's special counsel to the president, Ruben Sandoval, which contained the following:

> *I am deeply concerned with the matters that you have brought to my attention regarding your recent inquiries as to how the victims of the Alton School Bus tragedy have been treated. I am especially concerned with reports of numerous donations to benefit the families that may not have reached their destination.*[187]

Mr. De Lara's concern over the donations and how they were being handled was such that he traveled to the nearby city of McAllen and held a press conference in which he criticized Mayor San Juanita Zamora. He had spoken to families who told him at previous meetings that the mayor had "insulted, abused, identified [them] as non-citizens and even threatened [them]." He then declared, "Our organization is not going to tolerate this kind of activity."[188] Ms. Zamora pointed out after hearing about the meeting that Mr. De Lara had not yet spoken to any city officials.[189] Her letter would go on to state the other reason for De Lara traveling to the Rio Grande Valley:

> *I am also concerned, as you indicated, with reports that the victims' families are being discouraged from obtaining their own personal representatives and/or attorneys. I also find deplorable the reports that some families may be actually being threatened if they bring any kind of legal action.*

> As I indicated to you before, you have my authority to continue investigation into these matters, and that, if necessary, should some of those reports prove to be true, I hereby instruct you to report those matters to the State Bar of Texas in Austin, and to the proper authorities not at the local level.
>
> I further instruct you to keep me advised of any and all developments.
>
> This letter from me to you is given as my special counsel and National Chairmen of the Centro Juridico. No one is authorized on behalf of LULAC, you or me, to solicit and further victimize these families.[190]

The last sentence regarding solicitation would be what Mr. De Lara would later use to defend himself from the criticism leveled toward him and attorney Ruben Sandoval. At the aforementioned presentation by De Lara in McAllen, he declared to the public that his organization was appalled to hear that lawyers were victimizing families and taking fees as high as 40 percent from the grieving families. He issued a challenge to all attorneys to only charge 30 percent. He also indicated that he was willing to set up an office in Alton or Mission to protect the families.[191]

It was the presence of the national leadership of LULAC that led to a conflict between the local and national chapters of the civil rights organization. Within the state of Texas, LULAC was split into seventeen different regions, with Noe Torres being the Rio Grande Valley district director and Augie Pena being the director of social services. It would be these two who later came into conflict with President Jose De Lara and his special counsel, Ruben Sandoval. The local chapter claimed that despite the letter De Lara wrote, the president had actually sent Mr. Sandoval down to Alton for the purpose of soliciting clients for financial gain. In a sense, they were not acting in the best interest of the families, as they claimed, but were only present to take advantage of the people like all the other lawyers.

In a legal brief submitted by Armando Lopez, the local chapter laid out its claims against Jose De Lara and Ruben Sandoval. The document pointed out that as soon as the tragedy occurred, the local chapter went into action, serving the community in any way it could, from counseling to advice as to what services were available to them. It then went on to describe the following:

> On or about September 23, 1989, at a LULAC State Board Meeting held in Laredo, Texas, Ruben Sandoval...approached Mr. Noe Torres and asked him if he could get some cases in Alton. Mr. Torres informed

> Sandoval that he could not help him. Not to be put off, Sandoval...again approached Torres via a long distance telephone call, to tell him that LULAC was interested in sending various funds to local councils, those in Torres' District included. During the conversation, Sandoval once more, requested that Torres get him some cases in Alton. In the ensuing period, Sandoval telephoned Torres several times, leaving messages for Torres to return his calls.[192]

The mention of money that was going to be handed out to different chapters within LULAC can be seen as a financial incentive for Torres to assist Mr. Sandoval with the solicitation of clients involved in the Alton Bus Crash. In fact, later in this episode, money handed out by De Lara, Sandoval and other members of the president's staff would be seen in a similar light by some individuals. The brief then went on to state:

> Shortly thereafter, Sandoval personally went to the Rio Grande Valley under the guise of conducting LULAC business and requested to meet with Mr. Torres. They met at the Holidome Hotel, in McAllen, Texas. Torres was reluctant to accept that Sandoval was there to conduct LULAC business. Sandoval then telephoned LULAC national president Jose Garcia De Lara...and asked him to impress on Torres that Sandoval was to be "helped" in his quest to sign contracts of representation with the families of victims because, after all, Mr. Sandoval had been very generous with regard to the financial problems affecting the LULAC national office....Torres informed De Lara that Sandoval was too late as most of the families had already retained lawyers.[193]

However, this still did not deter Sandoval. It must be noted that it is illegal for a lawyer to solicit someone who has already signed a contract with another lawyer, as Mr. Torres pointed out to the president. The families he was trying to get business from were already signed with lawyers. The brief would go on to claim:

> Sandoval tried to entice Torres by mentioning figures of $50,000 or 60,000 as compensation for the solicitation of cases....When Torres inquired of Sandoval as to how the money would be reported to the Federal Government, Sandoval told Torres not to worry about the Internal Revenue Service because Sandoval would arrange for a "legitimate" loan for Mr. Torres with Sandoval's bank....Sandoval would take care of the bank's debt.[194]

The brief went on to describe an effort by Sandoval to use a former client of his, Mary Rodriguez, to try to solicit clients, to no avail. He then turned to Jose De Lara to use his power to influence people and lend legitimacy to Mr. Sandoval's presence in the Rio Grande Valley. This brief explains De Lara's reason for penning the letter of October 9, 1989, his journey to the Valley and his presentation in McAllen. It would also go on to point out that while Mr. De Lara and associates were in the Valley, they visited four families, all of whom had already retained lawyers. The document affirmed, "They [the families] were all informed that attorneys could easily be fired if the family wasn't satisfied with them. Money was handed out to the families by Mrs. Salvatierra [national secretary and administrator]. Within a short period of time, Ruben Sandoval had acquired two Alton cases."[195]

In direct refutation to claims that Jose De Lara gave money to the families as a financial incentive to get clients to leave their attorneys and sign with Mr. Sandoval, De Lara issued another letter on June 19, 1991, stating in part:

> *On or about October 12, 1989 the LULAC national secretary and administrator Betty Salvatierra, the LULAC national chief of staff Cruz Chavira, and I traveled to the Valley to see the issue* [claims of exploitation of the families and funds donated to them] *first hand.... We visited several families, and received testimony of victimization. The three of us pitched-in a modest amount of money and donated it to the families based on need. As LULAC members, this was our "job," our obligations as Christians. Never did we mention the firing or the hiring of any attorney. These allegations are untrue, and I challenge anyone to ask the visited families.*[196]

Betty Salvatierra wrote her own letter in response to the allegations leveled against her and the other members of LULAC who accompanied Mr. De Lara to the Valley:

> *I personally put together a small sum of money which we distributed to the families we visited. We did at no time inform any one that attorneys could be hired or fired. That was not our purpose for visiting these families. We went for humanitarian purposes to see how we could alleviate the suffering of the families. We visited six families that day and gave each family no more than $150.00 as a LULAC gesture of kindness....It is my understanding than on numerous occasions the families we visited have*

all stated that never was any mention of attorneys made during our visit. I also understand that allegations have been made that we visited the families with the intention of soliciting clients for Mr. Ruben Sandoval. **This is utterly preposterous**. [Salvatierra's emphasis][197]

This controversy would come to a head in a lawsuit, a retaliatory lawsuit and an indictment of barratry as a result of two clients leaving their previous attorney and signing on with Mr. Ruben Sandoval, causing the previous attorneys to file suit against Mr. Sandoval and his law partner, James A. Perkins.

The law firm of Flores, Munoz, Hockema and Reed representing Juan F. Lopez and Imelda Lopez, whose daughter, Ruby Lopez, died in the Alton Bus Crash, filed a temporary injunction against Ruben Sandoval and James Perkins to cease all communication with the Lopez family. They accused the attorneys of allegedly stealing the Lopezes away from the firm. The firm had first been contracted to act on the behalf of the Lopezes in their suit against Valley Coca-Cola. They then claimed that Perkins and Sandoval interfered with the firm's representation of the family.[198] Mr. Perkins responded to the allegations by calling the firm "a bunch of crybabies." He also remarked, "I think it's a joke. Some lawyers are spoil sports. They don't have a suit. It's nothing more than harassment. I told them that when they called me whining about it. It's ludicrous, ridiculous and irresponsible for these so-called lawyers to be filing a b.s. lawsuit."[199]

The firm offered to drop the suit if Perkins and Sandoval released the family from the contract they signed with them. Robert Reed with the firm stated, "I regret that the Lopez's have been thrust in the center of the controversy between the lawyers. I wish they had been left alone."[200] Perkins responded that he had not been contacted by the Lopezes about the matter, and he added, "I know for a fact that they do not want those attorneys....But if they wish to terminate our services we will comply with their wishes."[201]

Perkins and Sandoval also responded with a countersuit in which they submitted a transcript of an interview they conducted with Juan and Imelda Lopez. The transcript began with the following:

> Mr. Sandoval: *"First let me ask you, Mr. Lopez and Mrs. Lopez do you have an attorney, today?"*
> Mr. Lopez: *"No."*
> Mr. Sandoval: *"Mrs. Lopez do you have an attorney?"*
> Mrs. Lopez: *"No."*

This question was important to establish that on November 6, 1989, when the interview was conducted, the Lopezes were not under contract with any attorney. In the unfolding interview, it is revealed that the family had contacted Sandoval and Perkins of their own volition and were not solicited by the attorneys. They also expressed prior to the interview in a letter dated October 22, 1989, that they had written a letter to the law firm of Flores, Munoz, Hockema and Reed canceling their service. They agreed to turn over the letter to Perkins and Sandoval. They wished to end their relationship with the law firm because the firm did not really communicate with them and because they did not agree to the percentages being charged. The Lopezes stated that they had spoken to other families who had lost family members and were involved in lawsuits and saw that their percentages were far lower than what they were being charged by the law firm. They went on to indicate to the law firm that they would be seeking other counsel. In the interview, Sandoval made sure to have the Lopezes stress that they were not influenced nor contacted by him or his associate in drafting the letter or seeking them as counsel.[202]

In their countersuit, Sandoval and Perkins issued a defense to all allegations leveled against them and the actions of De Lara and associates. They also took aim at Noe Torres and Augie Pena. In their brief, they stated that the group was issuing "false, defamatory and slanderous statements about Plaintiffs [Ruben Sandoval and James Perkins] to third party persons," calling the attorneys "deceitful, corrupt, dishonest" and stating that Sandoval "had been guilty of barratry." As part of their attack, they provided the court with the aforementioned interview with the Lopezes.[203]

This brief look into the infighting occurring within a well-respected civil rights organization that had long stood tall on its accomplishments serves as an example of the internal and external conflicts centered on the money that came with the name Coca-Cola, a billion-dollar company. The fact that a grieving family was caught up in a legal quagmire was a tragedy—one that played itself out more than once throughout this sad tale. In addition, criminal charges like that of barratry did make their way into the courts, and Ruben Sandoval found himself being charged with barratry.

BARRATRY AND LAWSUITS

Within the first year of the accident, the Hidalgo County District Attorney's Office investigated fifteen cases of barratry.[204] A grand jury eventually convened and subsequently indicted three lawyers and one legal assistant. The jury was faced with the fact that many witnesses were absent or could not be served.[205] One of those who escaped indictment was Wilfredo "Willie" Garcia, mentioned earlier. He cooperated with the District Attorney's Office and avoided any charges.[206] Another obstruction to gaining a barratry indictment was the fact that many of the best witnesses, the clients, rarely testified against the person who provided them with their financial windfall. The only conviction that emerged from the barratry hearings was that of the legal secretary,[207] Ms. Norma Lopez, who was convicted of one count of barratry and was sentenced to one year deferred adjudication, a sentence with which District Attorney Rene Guerra was less than pleased.[208] The lawyers were later disciplined by the state bar, but none lost his or her license over the offenses.[209]

The unusually large number of illegal solicitations linked with the Alton Bus Crash and the roof collapse of the Amigo store in Brownsville (an aging secondhand store that collapsed under heavy rains) led to a backlash of anti-lawyer sentiment in the Rio Grande Valley. In fact, several businesses in partnership with the Valley Chamber of Commerce managed to collectively accumulate $250,000 to begin a campaign against barratry in the Valley. The group sponsored commercials and printed bumper stickers reading, "Fairness, Yes, Greed, No! Stop Lawsuit Abuse."[210] For it was not only ambulance chasing that had gotten out of hand as a result of the accident; there was also an inordinate number of frivolous lawsuits.

Some of the most surprising lawsuits came from the rescuers. Members of the Alton Fire Department sued, claiming that they suffered mental anguish as a result of their response to the tragedy.[211] These firefighters were later fired by Mayor Salvador Vela and then rehired as per court order.[212] One police officer attempted to do the same, but his chief indicated that all he had done was deliver Gatorade to the scene. There was also the case of Border Patrol agent John R. Swyers, who sought $3.4 million from Coca-Cola for his response to the scene.[213]

However, rescuers were not the only ones to attempt to cash in. There were several bystanders who sued Coke for the mental anguish resulting from their viewing the rescue efforts.[214] Finally, there was the father who submitted a wrongful death suit for the daughter he had never seen (nor paid any child support toward).[215]

One story that really stands out was the case of the security guard hired by Valley Coca-Cola to protect Ruben Perez from threats of violence that had been leveled at him. Alexander Murillo, a twenty-one-year-old security guard employed by Wackenhut Corporation, reported to police that on October 30, 1989, at approximately 2:30 a.m., he was kidnapped and attacked by three masked individuals. He claimed that while he was guarding Ruben Perez's home, three men jumped him and attempted to set him on fire. The men fled when the guard was able to subdue one of his attackers. The police managed to find some "Molotov cocktails" at the scene of the crime. The guard subsequently admitted himself to the hospital to be checked out.[216]

From the onset of the report, investigators with the Hidalgo County Sheriff's Department had their suspicions. Chief Deputy Bob Davis and the other officers questioned Murillo's version of the story, asking, "Why would three guys go to the Perez home to seek revenge for the deaths of 21 kids, and precede to burn alive an innocent 21-year-old security guard after they had already subdued him? Out of all the discrepancies from the beginning the biggest one was, Why?"[217] The investigators attempted to re-create the attack, but the story just did not add up, prompting them to call for a lie detector test, which Murillo subsequently failed. As a result, Murillo was arrested for making false statements to the police.[218] This story was an attempt by Murillo, like others, to later sue Coca-Cola and gain some sort of financial profit. This is just another example of how all kinds of people attempted to profit from the tragedy.

On the other side of the coin, there were the lawsuits between the sued parties. Valley Coca-Cola pointed out that it was not the only one responsible for the deaths. The company believed that the bus manufacturer, Blue Bird Bus Company, was also at fault for designing a bus from which it was difficult to escape.[219] However, Mission CISD spokesman Harlan Woods noted, "The 1985 Blue Bird bus seats 83 and had all the standard safety features required by state."[220] However, what Valley Coca-Cola was attempting to do was to include Blue Bird as a "third party defendant" in which some of the costs of the wrongful death suits would be deferred to them. Valley Coca-Cola also attempted to force the opposing legal teams to produce affidavits that proved the families had retained their legal counsel, but this was denied them.[221] Aside from those lawsuits filed against the bus manufacturer, there were suits filed against the former owners of the caliche pit; Corpus Christi Road Paving Company, the pavers of the intersection; Ballenger Construction; and the Mission School District.[222]

After all was said and done, millions were paid out. The lawyers earned more than $50 million from the Coca-Cola suits alone.[223] The families of the dead received from Coca-Cola about $4.5 million for each child lost, and the survivors were awarded settlements ranging from $500,000 to $900,000 from the soft drink manufacturer. Blue Bird Bus Company paid out $950,000 for each of the children whose lives were lost in the accident.[224] This was a huge financial windfall but generated some expected feelings and reactions. However, these emotions were amplified by the fact that the money came with such a high cost: the lives of their children, friends and family. Many of Alton's families felt guilt and remorse, as did many of the survivors.

PART III
AFTERMATH

SURVIVORS AND COMMUNITY

One of the survivors, Blanca Vargas, who was plagued early on by nightmares, stated to reporters, "I don't feel guilty because we all die. I feel bad because some lived and others didn't."[225] Peter Regalado, who lost two of his sisters in the accident, refused to move into the new home built in front of his small wooden home, explaining, "I just wish my sisters were here and we didn't get the settlement. What's the point of having everything you want if you're not happy?"[226] Two years after the accident, Rolando Ramon Jr., who lost two of his friends, David and Michael Saenz, still visited their house and just sat with their parents.[227] It was a singular act that helped fill the void of what both the boy and the parents had lost. This was the prevalent sentiment of the family members who lost so much as a result the tragedy.

For other survivors, this heartache has been so jarring that they have difficulties dealing with it to this day, whether it is driving past the site of the accident or seeing a school bus. Ms. Dora Rodriguez lost her sixteen-year-old daughter, Anna Delia Rodriguez. When she heard the accident, she ran out to see what happened and has never reentered her home. She left to stay with relatives, who retrieved her belongings. Even decades after the accident, she still panics when she hears a siren.[228]

For Maria G. Regalado, the mother of Lupina and Apolonia, the connection with her and her daughters was so great that with them gone, she shut herself off, refusing to talk much to others and not allowing music to be played in the house. She would constantly be worried anytime any of her other children left the house. Her daughter Maria said that she and the rest of the family grew worried for her health, and she eventually did have a heart attack from the emotional strain of the loss. She is still on heart medication to this day. Maria (the sister) stated in her interview that at the time of the accident she was nine months pregnant and that her sisters were excited to meet the baby, who was born one week after the accident. Maria went on to explain that ever since her baby was born, he would always get upset at the sound of sirens. Perhaps the anxiety of that day was passed on to the baby.

In the usual Mexican/Mexican American fashion, the bus crash inspired a *corrido* (a song that tells a story about an event, a tragedy or a hero/anti-hero), entitled "*La Tragedia en Mission*" ("The Tragedy in Mission") and written by Ray Salinas, who was still dealing with the death of his own son two years before. The inspiration came to him as he drove by the pit, and the lyrics began to compose themselves in his mind. An English translation of one of the verses reads, "One Thursday in the morning, the ambulances were crying, because they wanted to rescue the students who were drowning." The minute the song hit the airwaves, there were more than two hundred requests for the song, a testament to how many people were touched with the loss of twenty-one innocent lives.[229]

However, these feelings of sorrow were either not perceived or were ignored by some within the community of Alton, which led to rifts that exist to this day. Indeed, many in Alton saw their friends and neighbors profiting from their losses. In the words of former mayor San Juanita Zamora, "The crash ripped apart the city. The city is divided to the point I don't know if the city will ever be able to work together again."[230] Many felt a new distance from their friends and neighbors who now looked at them with envy and, in some cases, anger. There was even envy among some of the families of the victims. The parents of Jose Luis Ortega were the first family to settle and received $1.5 million for their loss, but when they found out that the rest of the families received $4.5 million, they filed suit to collect the other $3 million they felt was owed to them.[231] Moreover, there was even envy among the clergy of the Valley. As Reverend Samuel Arizpe of Alton's San Martin de Porres Catholic Church revealed, other priests from the surrounding parishes told him that now that many of the members of his community were millionaires, he should build a new church.[232]

Tragically, animosity occurred even within a family. Alexander De Leon running off and signing with his own attorney led to a huge rift within his family. Before he actually had a settlement, he was taking advance after advance, and in the end, when he received his settlement of $500,000 minus his advances and the 40 percent lawyer's fee, he was left with just $267,000. By the year 1997, he had spent all his money. He was divorced and estranged from his family. He explained, "I regret a lot—I went through money, partied, did drugs and it was crazy all this money coming in. But then when there is nothing left, you didn't invest it was gone." In time, he was able to reconnect with his mother, and their relationship is very strong. Her love has brought him back to reality and away from his previous vices. Sadly, the relationship with his sister still remains a bit strained, but in time hopefully that will heal as well.[233]

The siblings and survivors had their college tuitions paid for. Many of the families had family in Mexico whom they helped, building them houses and assisting financially.[234] The Alton church was indeed renovated by donations from the families.[235] Victims felt their world turned upside down with the loss of their children and how they were perceived differently by their friends and neighbors. Margarita Ortega, who lost her fifteen-year-old son, Jose, reflected the feelings of many: "We want them to treat us like before, but they can't. We feel poorer now than we were before, because we were happier then."[236]

Some of the behavior of the survivors and their families only served to spread rumors and resentment. On March 30, 1992, at 2:10 a.m., two of the survivors of the bus accident, Joe Vargas and Efrain Cruz, were killed when Vargas's 1992 Camaro IROC smashed into a tree.[237] Vargas's body was later found to contain alcohol and cocaine.[238] Yet another survivor, a few years after that tragedy, lost his leg in another drunk driving accident. Others descended into drugs and alcohol, quickly going through their millions.[239] But this is only half the story.

As for Ruben Perez, in the initial days after the accident, Coca-Cola hired security guards to protect him from the numerous death threats he received.[240] Perez then spent seven weeks in a psychiatric hospital following the crash.[241] Ruben spent the years following his acquittal in a "self-imposed home confinement" in which he ate, slept and lived in his bedroom.[242] Upon the twentieth anniversary of the accident in 2009, many reporters attempted to obtain an interview, but his whereabouts at the time were unknown.[243]

A memorial garden has been built at the site of the accident in which stands a monument that reads, "To everything there is a season and a time to every purpose under heaven," as well as a plaque that displays the names of the victims of the accident. There are twenty-one palms growing around the park, one for each victim.[244] Perhaps the most fitting tribute is Alton Memorial Middle School, which is named in memory of the lost children.[245] Yet for the people of Alton, the scars and the memories remain, from its exploitation by unscrupulous lawyers to the jealousy and greed. It was a tragedy that compounded exponentially.

Aftermath

This page, top: Right side of the Alton Memorial. *Courtesy of Jack Bloodworth.*

This page, bottom: Road sign for the park that is adjacent to the accident site. *Courtesy of Jack Bloodworth.*

Opposite, top: Alton Memorial. *Courtesy of Jack Bloodworth.*

Opposite, bottom: Left side of the Alton Memorial. *Courtesy of Jack Bloodworth.*

Photo of the park that is adjacent to the accident site. The existence of the park so close to the accident site is still somewhat controversial among residents. *Courtesy of Jack Bloodworth.*

The caliche pit today. *Photo by the author.*

Aftermath

CHANGES

It is a sad fact that there are probably hundreds if not thousands of issues in our world that have the potential for causing injury or even loss of life. Because business practices are governed by cost-benefit analyses, companies and manufacturers play the odds as to whether a tragedy will occur and, if so, how often. How much will they have to pay out? Is it cheaper than making changes? We have seen this in everything from pharmaceutical companies to the automotive industry. Unfortunately, when that loss of life occurs in such tragic circumstances, change finally comes for the safety of others. But it does little to bring people back nor ease the pain of those left behind. When it came to the bus crash in Alton, change did come.

Senator Carlos Truan of Corpus Christi introduced a bill requiring guardrails around any open pits near roadways.[246] The bill, passed in 1991, forced companies to erect barriers around any open pits or face fines of $10,000. This would be enforced by the Railroad Commission of Texas.[247] This permanently shifted the responsibility of pit safety to the company that either created it or continues to use it. Before the accident, Alton attempted to deal with the problem; however, if a law had existed, the tragedy could have prevented, and the responsibility of shifting blame from city to county to state could have been avoided.

The bus students ride today is designed with the Alton Bus Crash and the work of the Lansing Area Safety Council Operation STAR II, conducted in 1994, in mind. Bill Carter was a member of the council and described the reasoning behind the experiments they conducted. Speaking on crashes that result in a vehicle landing in a body of water, "Cars float for a few minutes before they go under. But the school buses plunge right to the bottom—boom. When they hit the bottom the windshield just collapses and the water rushes in. The thing sinks within 10 seconds."[248] In their experiments, they dropped a school bus full of mannequins thirty-four feet into the water of the Straits of Mackinac. They were able to see why buses sink as fast they do and what changes could be enacted to help to prevent a similar tragedy. The result of their experiments, motivated by the Alton Bus Crash, is that buses have been modified to promote rapid egresses from new exits. Buses now have exits on the roofs and on the sides, windows are now bigger and exit doors are now manufactured in such a way that they will open regardless of the effects of gravity (meaning no matter which direction a bus ends up facing after an accident).[249]

The Alton Bus Crash

Hoisted by a large crane, the school bus emerges from the caliche pit on the afternoon of Thursday, Sept. 21, 1989.

Tragedy results in safety changes

By ALLIE JOHNSON
©The Monitor

ALTON — When a Dr Pepper truck smashed into a loaded school bus 10 years ago, sending the bus tumbling 40 feet into a water-filled caliche pit, no one died of crash-related injuries.

But 21 of the junior high and high school students drowned because they could not get out of the submerged bus in time.

That left the angry, grieving community asking why there were not bigger windows and more emergency exits on the bus, and why measures were not taken to fill or fence the gaping caliche pits scattered around Hidalgo County.

In the decade since the accident, safety changes have been made, some as a direct result of the tragedy.

"In safety, you have to identify a problem, then work on it from there," said Bill Carter, of the Lansing Area Safety Council in Michigan, who knows exactly what happens when a school bus sinks.

Carter worked on a project in 1994 called Operation STAR II, inspired in part by the Alton bus accident, in which 11 school buses carrying crash test dummies were launched off a bridge into 34-foot-deep water in the Straits of Mackinac.

The findings were disturbing.

"Cars float for a few minutes before they go under," Carter said. "But the school buses plunge right to the bottom — boom. When they hit the water, the windshield just collapses and the water rushes in. The thing sinks within 10 seconds."

In the case of the Alton bus, the National Transportation Safety Board estimated that the bus sank in less than a minute. It quickly filled with water through the hole where the windshield had been.

In the pitch-dark water, students had trouble keeping the rear emergency exit open, and one student told the NTSB, according to their accident report, that she had tried to follow other students out of the emergency exit, but it slammed on her. She eventually escaped through a window.

Other students had trouble finding the emergency exits, and some larger students could not exit through the windows; most of the dead were found toward the center of the bus, far from the rear exit or the windshield area, the report said.

If such a rare accident were to happen today, the students would have many more ways out of the bus, Mission school district officials said.

"The exit doors are all designed to prop open regardless of gravity," said school district spokesman Craig Verley. "That was a direct result of the Alton accident."

The buses also have more emergency exits — the rear exit, two on each side and some on the roof, he said.

But the Alton bus would not have ended up in 12 feet of water if not for the caliche pit at Bryan Road and Five Mile Line. The abandoned pits are a result of excavation of caliche, a gravel-like material used in road construction.

According to a spokesman from the Railroad Commission of Texas, which regulates surface mining, the state Legislature in 1991 passed restrictions on open excavation pits — a direct result of the Alton accident.

The operators of abandoned quarries or pits now can be fined $10,000 for failing to "erect an approved safety barrier or slope or backfill (it) to eliminate the hazard," according to documents from the commission.

In 1989, *The Monitor* reported that the city of Alton had asked Hidalgo County to erect a barrier around the pit months before the accident, but county officials had denied the request, saying the state should pay.

Now, a tall chain link fence surrounds the pit in Alton where the children died.

The Monitor newspaper article on changes that resulted from the Alton school bus accident. *From* The Monitor, *September 22, 1999.*

Aftermath

On October 3, 2018, in Mesquite, Texas, a bus carrying forty-two Mesquite ISD students had its rear wheels veer off the road into some grass, causing the driver, John Johnson, to overcorrect, sending the bus into oncoming traffic. The driver then quickly tried to steer the bus back into the correct lane, sending the bus off the road again, onto its side and into a utility pole. The pole and its live wire coursing with electricity fell down onto the bus, causing it to burst into flames.[250] The students, with the help of bystanders, managed to exit the vehicle both through the back emergency door exit and the rooftop hatches.[251] Despite everyone's best efforts, one child, twelve-year-old Jazmine Alfaro, lost her life that day. However, the other children lived, some of whom survived thanks to emergency hatches that had been placed on the roof of the bus because twenty-one children died in a caliche pit in Alton, Texas.

CONCLUSION

Today, Alton is one of the fastest-growing cities in the Rio Grande Valley. It has even surpassed the populations of other cities in the Valley like Donna and Mercedes.[252] However, the scars of 1989 still linger, mostly due to many people who remained in the city and because of its small size. Everyone has driven by the memorial with a statue of Jesus with outstretched arms and both twenty-one palms and twenty-one wooden crosses with the names of those lost that Thursday morning. Nearby, adjacent to the memorial, is a public park. A chain link fence keeps people from entering the actual pit, but walking up close to the fence gets you pretty close to the site of the accident, which still has water emptying into it when it rains. From time to time, nearby residents and survivors who have returned to the pit have pointed out that different objects from the day of the accident have made their way to the surface or have been exposed by receding waters. These objects vary from bus seats to school supplies. Perhaps one day there can be a professional dig of the area to see what artifacts they can uncover from that sad day.

The adjacent park is problematic to survivors. Alex remarked that at the park, there are concerts and big parties being thrown, and "stuff like that just doesn't feel right."[253] These same sentiments were echoed in the days that passed when there was public discussions at city hall about what to do with the funds. Is it a dishonor to the dead to have these types of activities so close to where the accident happened? Especially when these events have no connection whatsoever to that fateful day. These are some of the many

Conclusion

questions that will continue to plague the city of Alton as it grows and evolves from its humble roots in the early 1900s.

There is no doubt that the accident left marks on all those who were touched by it, from passersby to rescuers, reporters, victims, families, teachers and local, county, state and national politicians. One sad note pointed out at the time of the accident is that then Texas governor Bill Clements did not spend any time in Alton, although he did send an investigative team. Nonetheless, the governor did come down during the Mark Kilroy incident, and some locals saw this as having to do with race and class. Mark Kilroy came from a well-off white family, but the children who were the victims in this catastrophe came from poor Mexican American homes.

Regarding the investigations by national and state authorities that were utilized so well by the defense, both sides did their best to establish what happened on the day of the crash. The highly scientific methods yielded results, but in the end, for the jury whose responsibility it was to provide a conviction, it was not the scientific testimony; the jury simply saw a lack of probable cause. Mr. Perez did not set out nor want to bring any harm to the kids. Whether it was faulty maintenance, not enough training or just sheer panic when the accident occurred, it was apparent to the jury and some of the survivors that it was an accident—a heinously tragic one, but an accident nonetheless.

The story of what happened to LULAC is a case study of greed and infighting, the likes of which almost overshadowed the loss of twenty-one innocent lives. The investigations into the motives behind the national president, his lawyer and the local chapters came to such a head that De Lara actually had to briefly dissolve the organization and restructure it financially as a result of missing monies that were discovered during the course of the investigation. One note on the claims made about bribery to change attorneys: it would seem that when lawyers are offering advances, like Alex De Leon's advance of $10,000, there would only be a little. There probably was more to the reasoning why there were shifts from one attorney to another than what was claimed in the press and the courts, but like other questions, this may remain unanswered.

The level of barratry and greed resulting from the bus crash rose to astonishing levels, along with the many families being taken advantage of by lawyers and their runners. Many of these families were inundated with strangers who were approaching people experiencing the worst calamity they had ever endured in their lives. Then these strangers showed up, seemingly

Conclusion

having their best interests in mind but having them sign documents many could not read, and even if they could read them, these people had never faced a civil lawsuit before in their lives. Consequently, they did not know which fees were fair and which were not. When it came to the rescue, one saw the best in humanity, but when it came to lawsuits and money, the worst in humanity reared its ugly head.

As mentioned in the introduction, the feeding frenzy of lawyers seeking high payouts was already present in the Valley with the collapse of the Amigo store in Brownsville, Texas, the year before, and it continued with the Alton Bus Crash. Soon after these events, the Rio Grande Valley would be known in legal circles as the lawsuit capital of the nation, a place where juries would pay out high sums. Since the time of the accident, the courts in the Valley have seen multimillion-dollar lawsuits dealing with the drug Vioxx and Goodyear tires.

Valley Coca-Cola's involvement in this whole affair can be seen in two different lights. The accident and the subsequent investigations revealed that there were lax maintenance issues in its delivery division, but there had been no other major accidents caused by its trucks. That is not to say that because of the accident, it caught others before those accidents happened. Despite the problems discovered in maintenance and upkeep, the corporation did appear to respond honorably after the accident, from ceasing advertising to sending Ms. Julie Martinez out to the neighborhoods with her ledger and company checkbook. The company paid for funerals, medical expenses and psychiatric treatment. Ms. Martinez's interview revealed nothing but shock and horror on the part of her employers, who sought to do whatever they could do to help the situation. The internal memos in Ms. Martinez's possession reveal no coverup nor dodging of corporate responsibility in the situation.

Finally, the victims of the accident, those who sat down to be interviewed about their experience, were very open about what happened to them during and after the accident. Their eyes and the way they sat spoke volumes. They sat still, almost unmoving, for most of the interview. Their eyes revealed that as they spoke they were transported back to that tragic moment in their minds, as did their tears—the tears for those they lost, the fact that they survived when others did not, their loss of innocence or, like in Alex De Leon's case, the family who were nearly torn apart. These rifts appeared as the community changed from a close-knit one to one with some distrust, as some were suddenly wealthy and some were not. Some used their settlements wisely and attended universities and even law school. Nevertheless, they are

Conclusion

all bound together by the terrible events of that day. The crosses that sit at the memorial are for their friends, classmates and relatives, and those young faces will always remain in their hearts and minds.

Throughout this book, the word *tragedy* has been used over and over, yet when a word like that is applied too much, it begins to lose its emotional sting. However, the loss of a child, a friend, a relative or a student is something one can never truly get over. It hits you when you see an empty seat, reach for a phone or want to share a tidbit of your life with the one person you always held close. What happened in Alton, Texas, on September 21, 1989, was a tragedy in the truest sense of the word.

Indeed, this event was a "compounded tragedy," in which there was not only loss of life but also rifts created, greed exposed and relationships estranged, showing how deep the wound was in Alton. The events exposed all that there is in humanity, the good and the bad. Like a Greek tragedy, it explores our humanity and exposes it before us for all to see. We feel the pain of loved ones lost and the anger of a small community that was exploited by others. The fact that some good has come of it and that possibly countless lives have been and will be saved due to the changes that were enacted because of the accident reveals that in the end, the prevailing truth is that there is more good in humanity than bad.

The main loss in this whole tragic affair is all the possibility that disappeared that day. In that bus and in those hospital beds, twenty-one potential doctors, lawyers, artists, scientists, lawmakers, leaders and more were lost. There is no telling the things these children could have produced, the families they could have created and the greater mark they could have left on the world. This is not to say their lives were lost in vain. Their families' lives are full of great memories and good times had with their loved ones, and these are the most precious things, far greater than money. They also led to safety measures that protect today's children.

When all is said and done, the image that remains with this author is that of bright-eyed children at the bus stop, laughing and chatting with one another. At bus stops everywhere, there stands our future and the hopes and dreams of parents everywhere.

NOTES

Introduction

1. City of Alton, "History of Alton, Texas."
2. Alonzo, *Tejano Legacy*, 149.
3. City of Alton, "History of Alton, Texas."
4. Ibid.
5. Ibid.
6. De Leon interview by Zavala and Carmona.
7. Ibid.
8. Wells, "Brownsville Texas Building Collapse."
9. Exponent Engineering and Consulting Firm, "Building Collapse After Structural Modification."
10. Martinez, "La Tienda Amigo Fell Down."
11. Cartwright, "Work of the Devil."
12. Hernandez interview by Carmona.
13. Cartwright, "Work of the Devil."
14. Findlaw, "Compulsory Education Laws."

Part I

15. National Transportation Safety Board, "Highway Accident Report."
16. Ibid.

17. Ibid.
18. Ibid.
19. Ibid.
20. Cuellar interview by Zavala and Carmona.
21. National Transportation Safety Board, "Highway Accident Report."
22. Bragg and Rugeley, "They Were All Holy Innocents," 1A.
23. National Transportation Safety Board, "Highway Accident Report."
24. Flores interview by Lavendera.
25. National Transportation Safety Board, "Highway Accident Report."
26. Ibid.
27. Larson, "Alton Had Sought Barrier," 1A, 8A.
28. Flores interview by Lavendera.
29. Ibid.
30. Sralla, "Helper Recounts Bus Crash," 1A.
31. Flores interview by Lavendera.
32. De Leon interview by Zavala and Carmona.
33. National Transportation Safety Board, "Highway Accident Report."
34. Romero, "Last Student to Board Bus," 2A.
35. National Transportation Safety Board, "Highway Accident Report."
36. Flores interview by Lavendera.
37. De Leon interview by Zavala and Carmona.
38. Wittmann "Matrix Effect."
39. Bragg and Rugeley, "They Were All Holy Innocents," 1A.
40. National Transportation Safety Board, "Highway Accident Report."
41. Marisele Ortega quoted in Bragg and Rugeley, "19 Children Die," Sec. A.
42. Flores interview by Lavendera.
43. Cuellar interview by Zavala and Carmona.
44. Bragg and Rugeley, "19 Children Die," 1A.
45. De Leon interview by Zavala and Carmona.
46. Cuellar interview by Zavala and Carmona.
47. Bragg and Rugeley, "19 Children Die," Sec. A.
48. Flores, "Cheerleader Administers CPR to Save Best Friend," 1A.
49. Action 4 News, "Woman Recalls Missing Alton School Bus."
50. De Leon interview by Zavala and Carmona.
51. Larson and Guevara, "Lawsuits Filed," Sec. A, 7.
52. Cullick, "Brother's Love Led to His Death," 15A.
53. Shannon, "Rescue Efforts Recalled," Sec. A, 8.
54. Bragg and Rugeley, "They Were All Holy Innocents," 1A.

55. De Leon interview by Zavala and Carmona.
56. Roque Sosa quoted in Bragg and Rugeley, "They Were All Holy Innocents," 1A.
57. Bragg and Rugeley, "They Were All Holy Innocents," 1A.
58. Romero, "Last Student to Board Bus," 2A.
59. *The Monitor*, "Passerby Aided in Rescue," 1A.
60. Nichols and McLemore, "Two Families Suffer Double Loss," 15A.
61. Maria Regalado interviewed by Juan Carmona.
62. Nichols and McLemore, "Two Families Suffer Double Loss," 15A.
63. Ibid.
64. Omar Botello quoted in Cullick and Rugeley, "Torn Asunder."
65. *Brownsville Herald*, "Memories of Alton School Bus Crash Linger," 2A.
66. *The Monitor*, "Firefighter Saves at Least 10."
67. Larson, Romero and Ramirez, "20th Bus Crash Victim," 1A, 8A.
68. Ibid., 8.
69. *Los Angeles Times*, "19 Youngsters Die."
70. Fatherree, "Rescue Workers Get Shots," 1.
71. Larson, "Scholarship Fund Started," 10A.
72. De Leon interview by Zavala and Carmona.
73. Ruiz interview by Zavala and Carmona.
74. Ibid.
75. Ibid.
76. Eilts interview by Zavala and Carmona.
77. *The Monitor*, "Victims of Crash Identified," 1A.
78. Quintanilla interview by Carmona.
79. *Houston Chronicle*, "18 Dead, 47 Hurt," 1A.
80. KGBT-TV Channel 4, "KGBT Archives: Alton Bus Crash Original Report."
81. Cullick and Rugeley, "Torn Asunder," 1A.
82. Williams, "Death Toll in Texas' Worst School Bus Accident," 1A.
83. Bragg, "Valley Grieves for Bus Crash Victims," 1A.
84. Roebuck, "Even After Two Decades," 3A.
85. Ratcliffe, "School Bus Tragedy," 1A.
86. Romero, "Committee Will Decide," 1A.
87. Williams, "Death Toll in Texas' Worst School Bus Accident," 1A.
88. Martinez interview Zavala and Carmona.
89. Julie Martinez, private papers.
90. Ibid.
91. Guevara, "Blank Check," 9A.

92. Ibid.
93. Bragg and Rugeley, "They Were All Holy Innocents," 1A.
94. KRGV-TV News 5, "Special Report: Alton Bus Crash."
95. KGBT-TV Channel 4, "KGBT Archives: Alton Bus Crash Memorial Service."
96. Powell "30 Years Ago Today."
97. Larson, "Counselors Ready to Help Survivors," 1A.
98. Larson, "Scholarship Fund Started," 1A.
99. Ibid., 10A.
100. Dr. Igoa quoted in Larson, "Counselors Ready to Help Survivors," 8A.
101. Larson, "Counselors Ready to Help Survivors," 8A.
102. Cullick and Bragg, "9,000 Join to Grieve for Kids," 1A.
103. KRGV Channel 5 News, "Alton 20th Anniversary."
104. Cullick and Bragg, "9,000 Join to Grieve for Kids," 1A.
105. Williams, "Saddened Students to Return Today," 10A.
106. Rojas interview by Carmona.
107. Williams, "Saddened Students to Return Today," 10A.
108. *Valley Morning Star*, "Students Return, Face Empty Desks," 1A.
109. Ibid., 10A.
110. John Abbenante quoted in *Valley Morning Star*, "Students Return, Face Empty Desks," 1A.
111. Pat Gilton quoted in *Valley Morning Star*, "Students Return, Face Empty Desks," 1A.
112. Larson, "Flyer Targets Alton Mayor," 1A.
113. Romero, "Crowd Calls for Alton Mayor to Quit," 10A.
114. Ibid.
115. Larson, "Flyer Targets Alton Mayor," 1A.
116. Ibid.
117. Bragg, "Valley Grieves for Bus Crash Victims," 1A.
118. Bragg and Rugeley, "They Were All Holy Innocents," 1A.
119. Bragg, "Valley Grieves for Bus Crash Victims," 1A.
120. Rugeley, "Trailer Brakes Work," 1A.
121. Robinson, "Truck in Bus Wreck," 1A.
122. Lee Dickinson quoted in Robinson, "Truck in Bus Wreck," 1A.
123. Robinson, "Truck in Bus Wreck," 1A.
124. Ibid.
125. Representative Mark Stiles (D) quoted in Robinson, "Truck in Bus Wreck," 1A.
126. Robinson, "Truck in Bus Wreck," 1A.

NOTES TO PAGES 63–74

127. Ibid
128. National Transportation Safety Board, "Highway Accident Report."
129. Ibid.
130. *Houston Chronicle*, "Truck Driver Pleads Innocent," 1A.
131. *Houston Chronicle*, "Public Inquiry Urged," 1A.
132. McDonald, "Feds Won't Set Hearing," 1A.
133. Guevara, "Report Gets Mixed Reactions," 1A.

Part II

134. Guerra interview by Carmona.
135. Larson, "Perez Indicted in Bus Accident," 1, 12A.
136. Olivia Hernandez quoted in Larson, "Perez Indicted in Bus Accident," 12A.
137. Rene Guerra quoted in Larson, "Perez Indicted in Bus Accident," 12A.
138. Larson, "Perez Indicted in Bus Accident," 12A.
139. Ibid., 12A.
140. Blakeslee, "Worst Judges in Texas."
141. Ibid.
142. Rick Diaz quoted in Sralla, "Judge Demands Personal Mention," 1A.
143. Sralla, "Judge Demands Personal Mention," 1A.
144. Jeff Koch quoted in Sralla, "Judge Demands Personal Mention," 1A.
145. Fidencio Guerra quoted in Sralla, "Judge Demands Personal Mention," 1A.
146. *Brownsville Herald*, "Both Sides Haggle."
147. Garcia, "Jury Selection Begins," 1A, 2A.
148. Rene Guerra quoted in Garcia, "Jury Selection Begins," 1A, 2A.
149. Joseph Connors quoted in Garcia, "Jury Selection Begins," 1A, 2A.
150. Garcia, "Jurors Chosen for Perez Trial Mostly Women," 1A.
151. *New York Times*, "Driver Acquitted of Homicide."
152. Sralla, "Judge Throws Out Manslaughter Counts," 1A, 12A.
153. NTSB "Accident."
154. Sralla, "Attorney Arguments Get Fierce," 1A.
155. Sralla, "Judge Throws Out Manslaughter Counts," 1A.
156. Lemieux, "Details Bog Down Alton Bus Crash Trial."
157. Sralla, "Witness: Perez Anguished," 1A, 6A.
158. Arturo Garza quoted in Sralla, "Witness: Perez Anguished," 1A, 6A.
159. Sralla, "Witness: Perez Anguished," 6A.

160. Joseph Connors quoted in Sralla, "Helper Recounts Bus Crash," 1A, 10A.
161. Sralla, "Judge Throws Out Manslaughter Counts," 1A.
162. *New York Times*, "Driver Acquitted of Homicide."
163. Pinkerton, "Acquitted Driver Seeks Recompense," 1A.
164. *New York Times*, "Driver Acquitted of Homicide."
165. Lemieux, "Details Bog Down Alton Bus Crash Trial."
166. Sralla, "Expert: Delivery Truck," 6A.
167. Ibid., 1A.
168. Dan Asa quoted in Sralla, "Expert: Delivery Truck," 1A.
169. Dan Asa quoted in Sralla, "Improper Maintenance Blamed," 1C.
170. Sralla, "Improper Maintenance Blamed," 2C.
171. Lemieux, "Alton Bus Crash Trial."
172. *KRGV Channel 5 News*, "Alton 20th Anniversary."
173. Yolanda Lopez interview by Carmona.
174. Lemieux, "Driver Perez Hopes."
175. Roebuck, "Bitter Divorce Battle."
176. Ibid.
177. Ibid.
178. Ibid.
179. Marcotte, "Barratry Indictments," 21.
180. Williams, "18 Lawyers Investigated," 1A.
181. Marcotte, "Barratry Indictments," 21.
182. Pinkerton and Bragg, "3 Lawyers Go to Court," 1A.
183. Williams, "Valley School Bus Accident," 1A.
184. De Leon interview by Zavala and Carmona.
185. Ibid.
186. LULAC, "History."
187. De Lara, "Letter to Ruben Sandoval."
188. De Lara quoted in Larson, "LULAC Official Criticizes Alton Mayor," 4A.
189. Larson "LULAC Official Criticizes Alton Mayor," 4A.
190. De Lara, "Letter to Ruben Sandoval."
191. Larson "LULAC Official Criticizes Alton Mayor," 4A.
192. Lopez, *James A. Perkins, Ruben Sandoval and Jose De Lara v. Augie Pena, Noe Torres and Mark Cantu*.
193. Ibid.
194. Ibid.
195. Ibid.

196. De Lara, "Open Letter."
197. Salvatierra "Open Letter."
198. Nettles, "Firm Fight Over Representation," 10A.
199. James Perkins quoted in Guevara, "Law Firm Charges."
200. Robert Reed quoted in Nettles, "Firm Fight Over Representation," 10A.
201. James Perkins quoted in Nettles, "Firm Fight Over Representation," 10A.
202. Juan Lopez and Ismelda Lopez interview by Sandoval.
203. Hall, "James A. Perkins and Ruben Sandoval."
204. Roebuck, "Even After Two Decades," 3A.
205. Pinkerton, "Indictments Charge Ambulance-Chasing," 1A.
206. Roebuck, "Bitter Divorce Battle."
207. Pinkerton, "Spoils of Tragedy," 1A.
208. Guevara, "Attorneys to Discuss Barratry Sentencing," 8A.
209. Pinkerton and Golightly, "Spoils of Tragedy," 1A.
210. Ibid.
211. Weiss, "America's Queen of Torts," 82.
212. Smith, "September Tragedy: Time and Money," 1A.
213. Lemieux, "350 Lawsuits Filed," 1A.
214. Weiss, "America's Queen of Torts," 82.
215. Roebuck, "Even After Two Decades," 2A.
216. Larson, "Attempt Made to Set on Fire," 1A.
217. Bob Davis quoted in Larson, "Guard Who Reported Attack."
218. Larson, "Guard Who Reported Attack."
219. Lemieux, "350 Lawsuits Filed," 1A.
220. Bragg and Robison, "Charges Possible in Alton Disaster," 1A.
221. Williams, "Bottling Firm Tied to Accident," 1A.
222. Pinkerton and Golightly, "Spoils of Tragedy," 1A.
223. Brezosky, "After 20 Years."
224. Roebuck, "Even After Two Decades," 2A.

Part III

225. Smith, "September Tragedy: In Sleep, Friends Return," 1A.
226. Smith, "September Tragedy: Time and Money," 1A.
227. Montes "Pain, Bad Memories Linger," 1A.
228. Long, "Stricken Mom Never Returned Home," 1A.

229. Larson, "Bus Crash Victims Recalled in Song," 1A.
230. Smith, "September Tragedy: Time and Money," 1A.
231. Pinkerton, "Spoils of Tragedy," 1A.
232. Smith, "September Tragedy: Time and Money," 1A.
233. De Leon interview by Zavala and Carmona.
234. Lemieux, "Settlement Money."
235. Roebuck, "Even After Two Decades," 2A.
236. Margarita Ortega quoted in Franke, "Alton Marks Fifth Anniversary of Bus Tragedy," 1A.
237. Pinkerton, "Two Alton Bus Crash Survivors," 1A.
238. Brezosky, "After 20 Years."
239. Roebuck, "Even After Two Decades," 2A.
240. Williams, "Driver in Alton Bus Crash," 1A.
241. Lemieux, "Man's Trial in Bus Crash," 1A.
242. Roebuck, "Even After Two Decades," 2A.
243. *KRGV Channel 5 News*, "Alton 20th Anniversary."
244. *Brownsville Herald*, "Archived Story: Alton Bus Crash Victims Remembered."
245. *KRGV Channel 5 News*, "Alton 20th Anniversary."
246. Bragg, "Valley Grieves for Bus Crash Victims," 1A.
247. Johnson, "Tragedy Results in Safety Changes," 5A.
248. Bill Carter quoted in Johnson, "Tragedy Results in Safety Changes," 5A.
249. Johnson, "Tragedy Results in Safety Changes," 5A.
250. Sivilay, "Report Reveals Cause."
251. *NBC 5*, "One Student Dies."

Conclusion

252. Capucion, "Alton Officials Expect."
253. De Leon interview by Zavala and Carmona.

BIBLIOGRAPHY

Action 4 News. "Woman Recalls Missing Alton School Bus that Crashed, Killing 21." YouTube, September 20, 2011. http://www.youtube.com/watch?v=3KM3Cw1SE5w&feature=related.

Alonzo, Armando C. *Tejano Legacy: Rancheros and Settlers in South Texas, 1734–1900*. Albuquerque: University of New Mexico Press, 1998.

Blakeslee, Nate. "The Worst Judges in Texas." *Texas Observer*, January 8, 2013. https://www.texasobserver.org/2132-the-worst-judges-in-texas-in-these-courtrooms-justice-comes-to-a-screeching-halt.

Bragg, Roy. "Valley Grieves for Bus Crash Victims. No Braking Trouble Seen in Bus Probe." *Houston Chronicle*, September 23, 1989.

Bragg, Roy, and Clay Robison. "Charges Possible in Alton Disaster." *Houston Chronicle*, September 22, 1989.

Brezosky, Lynn. "After 20 Years, Scars from Valley Bus Tragedy Remain." *Houston Chronicle*, September 20, 2009. http://www.chron.com/news/houston-texas/article/After-20-years-scars-from-Valley-bus-tragedy-1720128.php.

Brownsville Herald. "Archived Story: Alton Bus Crash Victims Remembered." Freedom Reports, December 31, 2012. http://www.brownsvilleherald.com/news/bus-25146-crash-cantu.html.

———. "Both Sides Haggle at Alton Bus Crash Hearing." April 3, 1993.

———. "Memories of Alton School Bus Crash Linger." September 20, 1999.

Bibliography

Capucion, Ena. "Alton Officials Expect Population to Hit 20,000 When 2020 Census Is Taken." *Rio Grande Guardian*, June 14, 2018. https://riograndeguardian.com/alton-officials-expect-population-to-hit-20000-when-2020-census-is-taken.

Cartwright, Gary. "The Work of the Devil." *Texas Monthly*, June 1, 1989. https://www.texasmonthly.com/articles/the-work-of-the-devil.

City of Alton. "History of Alton, Texas." April 2017. https://alton-tx.gov/wp-content/uploads/2017/04/History-of-Alton-Texas.pdf.

Cullick, Robert. "Brother's Love Led to His Death." *The Monitor*, September 22, 1989.

Cullick, Robert, and Cindy Rugeley. "Torn Asunder: Bus Death Wraps Town in Grief." *Houston Chronicle*, September 24, 1989.

Cullick, Robert, and Roy Bragg. "9,000 Join to Grieve for Kids. Tragedy Draws Community Closer." *Houston Chronicle*, September 23, 1989.

De Lara, Jose. "Letter to Ruben Sandoval." October 9, 1989.

———. "Open Letter." Found in Jose Garcia De Lara Papers, Benson Latin American Collection, University of Texas Libraries, the University of Texas–Austin, June 19, 1991.

Exponent Engineering and Consulting Firm. "Store Collapse After Structural Modification." 2018. https://www.exponent.com/experience/store-collapse-after-structural-modification/?pageSize=NaN&pageNum=0&loadAllByPageSize=true.

Fatherree, Tom. "Rescue Workers Get Shots." *The Monitor*, September 23, 1989.

Findlaw. "Compulsory Education Laws: Background." December 31, 2016. https://education.findlaw.com/education-options/compulsory-education-laws-background.html.

Flores, Veronica. "Cheerleader Administers CPR to Save Best Friend." *Brownsville Herald*, September 22, 1989.

Franke, Caitlin. "Alton Marks Fifth Anniversary of Bus Tragedy." *The Monitor*, September 22, 1994.

Garcia, Panfilo. "Jurors Chosen for Perez Trial Mostly Women." *The Monitor*, April 16, 1993.

———. "Jury Selection Begins in Alton Bus Crash Trial." *The Monitor*, April 14, 1994.

Guevara, Rey. "Attorneys to Discuss Barratry Sentencing." *The Monitor*, May 14, 1991.

———. "Law Firm Charges Bus Accident Clients Were Lured Away." Found in Jose Garcia De Lara Papers, Benson Latin American Collection, University of Texas Libraries, the University of Texas–Austin.

Bibliography

Guevara, Rey V. "Blank Check' Offered for Psychiatric Care." *The Monitor*, October 10, 1989.

———. "Report Gets Mixed Reactions." *The Monitor*, July 18, 1990.

Hall, Thomas C. "James A. Perkins and Ruben Sandoval v. Rafael H. Flores, Albert A. Munoz, Jr., David H. Hoekema, Roger H. Reed, Mark Cantu, Augie Pena and Noe Torres in the District Court 150th District Bexar County, Texas." Found in Jose Garcia De Lara Papers, Benson Latin American Collection, University of Texas Libraries, the University of Texas–Austin, 1989.

Houston Chronicle. "18 Dead, 47 Hurt After School Bus Plunges into Pit." September 21, 1989.

———. "Public Inquiry Urged in Alton Bus Crash. Board Members Seeking Safety Lessons." December 6, 1989.

———. "Truck Driver Pleads Innocent to Charges." November 23, 1989.

Johnson, Allie. "Tragedy Results in Safety Changes." *The Monitor*, September 22, 1999.

KGBT-TV Channel 4. "KGBT Archives: Alton Bus Crash Memorial Service." YouTube, September 18, 2011. http://www.youtube.com/watch?v=Run5z_z-fvA.

———. "KGBT Archives: Alton Bus Crash Original Report." YouTube, September 18, 2011. http://www.youtube.com/watch?v=uADLMoUplFM&feature=relmfu.

KRGV-TV News 5. "Special Report: Alton Bus Crash 20th Anniversary (Part 1)." YouTube, September 21, 2009. http://www.youtube.com/watch?v=5WE6BJjMkkg.

Larson, Jackie. "Alton Had Sought Barrier Along Caliche Pit." *The Monitor*, September 21, 1989.

———. "Attempt Made to Set on Fire Guard at Truck Driver's Home." *The Monitor*, October 30, 1989.

———. "Bus Crash Victims Recalled in Song." *The Monitor*, September 20, 1989.

———. "Counselors Ready to Help Survivors." *The Monitor*, September 25, 1989.

———. "Flyer Targets Alton Mayor." *The Monitor*, November 14, 1989.

———. "Guard Who Reported Attack at Truck Driver's Home Is Arrested." *The Monitor*, n.d.

———. "LULAC Official Criticizes Alton Mayor." *The Monitor*, October 14, 1989.

Bibliography

———. "Perez Indicted in Bus Accident." *The Monitor*, November 22, 1989.

———. "Scholarship Fund Started." *The Monitor*, September 27, 1989.

Larson, Jackie, and Rey Guevara. "Lawsuits Filed in Connection with the Alton School Bus Tragedy." *The Monitor*, October 4, 1989.

Larson, Jackie, Mariana Romero and Ivonne Ramirez. "20th Bus Crash Victim Dies as Federal Investigation Begins." *The Monitor*, September 23, 1989.

Lemieux, Josh. "Alton Bus Crash Trial to Go to Jury Wednesday." *Brownsville Herald*, December 31, 2017. http://www.brownsvilleherald.com/news/perez-45826-jury-truck.html.

———. "Details Bog Down Alton Bus Crash Trial." *Brownsville Herald*, April 23, 1993.

———. "Driver Perez Hopes to Turn Alton Bus Crash Trial Around." *Brownsville Herald*, December 31, 2017 https://www.brownsvilleherald.com/news/local/driver-perez-hopes-to-turn-alton-bus-crash-trial-around/article_c0448d96-d082-59eb-ac38-d3d1467fb9f1.html.

———. "Man's Trial in Bus Crash Set to Begin. Truck Driver Tied in Deaths of 21." *Houston Chronicle*, April 12, 1993.

———. "Settlement Money in '89 School Bus Accident Tears Town Apart: Many in the Small Community of Alton Are Upset that a Number of the 21 Victims' Families Have Used Lawsuit Money to Move into Bigger Houses and Buy Expensive Cars." *Los Angeles Times*, December 31, 1999. http://articles.latimes.com/1994-01-02/news/mn-7628_1_settlement-money.

———. "350 Lawsuits Filed Since '89 Bus Accident in Alton." *Houston Chronicle*, December 12, 1993.

Long, Cindy. "Stricken Mom Never Returned Home." *The Monitor*, September 21, 1999.

Lopez, Armando. *James A. Perkins, Ruben Sandoval and Jose De Lara v. Augie Pena, Noe Torres and Mark Cantu*. Case no. 89-CI-21029, 150th Judicial Court of Bexar County, Texas. Found in Jose Garcia De Lara Papers, Benson Latin American Collection, University of Texas Libraries, the University of Texas–Austin, 1989.

Los Angeles Times. "19 Youngsters Die in Crash of School Bus." December 31, 2005. http://articles.latimes.com/1989-09-21/news/mn-1129_1_school-bus-accident.

LULAC. "History." December 31, 2011. https://lulac.org/about/history.

Marcotte, Paul. "Barratry Indictments: DA Claims Four Texas Lawyers Solicited Bus-Crash Clients." *Journal of the American Bar Association*, no. 21 (1990).

BIBLIOGRAPHY

Martinez, Laura B. "La Tienda Amigo Fell Down 20 Years Ago This Month." *The Monitor*, July 13, 2008. https://www.themonitor.com/article_682c387b-b35b-50c6-8e9f-24e3e240a1ea.html.

McDonald, Gregg. "Feds Won't Set Hearing on Alton Crash." *Houston Chronicle*, December 7, 1989.

The Monitor. "Firefighter Saves at Least 10 at Crash Site." September 22, 1990.

———. "Passerby Aided in Rescue," September 21, 1989, 1A.

———. "Victims of Crash Identified." September 22, 1989.

Montes, Eduardo. "Pain, Bad Memories Linger in Alton." *Valley Morning Star*, September 20, 1991.

National Transportation Safety Board. "Highway Accident Report." NTSB no. HAR-90/2.NTIS no. PB90-916201. U.S. Department of Commerce National Technical Information Service, 1990.

NBC 5. "One Student Dies in Mesquite School Bus Crash: Counselors Are Available for Students and Staff at Terry Middle School." https://www.nbcdfw.com/news/local/Mesquite-ISD-School-Bus-Involved-in-Crash-495089881.html.

Nettles, Brenda. "Firm Fight Over Representation of Alton Family." *Valley Morning Star*, November 29, 1989.

New York Times. "Driver Acquitted of Homicide in School Bus Crash in Texas." May 7, 1993. http://www.nytimes.com/1993/05/07/us/driver-acquitted-of-homicide-in-school-bus-crash-in-texas.html?pagewanted=2&src=pm.

Nichols, Bruce, and David Mclemore. "Two Families Suffer Double Loss." *The Monitor*, September 21, 1989.

Pinkerton, James. "Acquitted Driver Seeks Recompense: Coca-Cola Being Sued Over Brakes." *Houston Chronicle*, May 7, 1993.

———. "Indictments Charge Ambulance-Chasing." *Houston Chronicle*, April 7, 1990.

———. "The Spoils of Tragedy. Barratry Brings One Horror After Another." *Houston Chronicle*, August 4, 1992.

———. "Two Alton Bus Crash Survivors Die in Accident." *Houston Chronicle*, March 31, 1992.

Pinkerton, James, and Glen Golightly. "The Spoils of Tragedy: Profiting on Disaster, Unscrupulous Lawyers Solicit Victims in Valley." *Houston Chronicle*, August 2, 1992.

Pinkerton, James, and Roy Bragg. "3 Lawyers Go to Court on Bus Wreck Barratry Charges." *Houston Chronicle*, April 10, 1990.

BIBLIOGRAPHY

Powell, Lisa. "30 Years Ago Today: Nation's Deadliest Drunken Driving Crash Involved Bus Returning from Kings Island." *My Dayton Daily News*, May 14, 2018. https://www.mydaytondailynews.com/news/local/years-ago-today-nation-deadliest-drunken-driving-crash-involved-bus-returning-from-kings-island/R95VbJ3sj0EJWyhjZyZIhO.

Ratcliffe, R.G. "School Bus Tragedy Ticket Giveaway Raises $50,000 for Crash Victims." *Houston Chronicle*, September 23, 1989.

Robinson, Clay. "Truck in Bus Wreck Had Bad Brakes." *Houston Chronicle*, October 6, 1989.

Roebuck, Jeremy. "Bitter Divorce Battle Reveals Unflattering Side of South Texas Legal System." *The Monitor*, June 27, 2010.

———. "Even After Two Decades, Wounds Still Divide Alton." *The Monitor*, September 20, 2009.

Romero, Mariana. "Committee Will Decide How to Use Money Donated in Tragedy." *The Monitor*, October 2, 1989.

———. "Crowd Calls for Alton Mayor to Quit." *The Monitor*, October 6, 1989.

———. "Last Student to Board Bus Recalls Disastrous Collision." *The Monitor*, September 25, 1989.

Rugeley, Cindy. "Trailer Brakes Work in Crash Re-Creation." *Houston Chronicle*, September 25, 1989.

Salvatierra, Betty. "Open Letter." Found in Jose Garcia De Lara Papers, Benson Latin American Collection, University of Texas Libraries, the University of Texas–Austin, n.d.

Shannon, Kelley. "Rescue Efforts Recalled." *The Monitor*, September 23, 1989.

Sivilay, Anny. "Report Reveals Cause of Mesquite Bus Crash." *Mesquite News*, October 5, 2018. https://starlocalmedia.com/mesquitenews/news/report-reveals-cause-of-mesquite-bus-crash/article_2e976484-c8cb-11e8-90b7-eb3318f1f301.html.

Smith, Mark. "A September Tragedy: In Sleep, Friends Return. Nightmare Beckons Survivor 'Come on, Let's Go.'" *Houston Chronicle*, September 16, 1990.

———. "A September Tragedy: Time and Money Haven't Ended Alton's Anguish." *Houston Chronicle*, September 16, 1990.

Sralla, Buck. "Attorney Arguments Get Fierce in Perez Trial." *The Monitor*, April 28, 1993.

———. "Expert: Delivery Truck Not Properly Maintained." *The Monitor*, April 29, 1993.

———. "Helper Recounts Bus Crash." *The Monitor*, April 20, 1993.

———. "Judge Demands Personal Mention." *The Monitor*, April 20, 1993.

———. "Judge Throws Out Manslaughter Counts, Reduces Charges in Perez Trial." *The Monitor*, April 24, 1993.

———. "Improper Maintenance Blamed for Bus Crash." *The Monitor*, April 30, 1993.

———. "Witness: Perez Anguished Over Fate of Kids." *The Monitor*, April 22, 1993.

Valley Morning Star. "Students Return, Face Empty Desks." September 26, 1989.

Weiss, Michael D. "America's Queen of Torts." *Policy Review*, no. 82 (Fall 1992).

Wells, John. "Brownsville Texas Building Collapse, 1988." YouTube, April 4, 2012. https://www.youtube.com/watch?v=5OY5yvBcsv8.

Williams, Joel. "Bottling Firm Tied to Accident that Killed 21 Sues Bus Maker." *Houston Chronicle*, January 30, 1990.

———. "Death Toll in Texas' Worst School Bus Accident Hits 21 as Girl 15, Dies." *Houston Chronicle*, September 30, 1989.

———. "Driver in Alton Bus Crash Received Threats." *Houston Chronicle*, September 28, 1989.

———. "18 Lawyers Investigated for Illegal Solicitation After Bus Accident." *Houston Chronicle*, November 18, 1989.

———. "Saddened Students to Return Today: Counselors Will Attend Classes; Parents Fear Busses." *Valley Morning Star*, September 25, 1989.

———. "Valley School Bus Accident Leads to 50 Lawsuits." *Houston Chronicle*, October 19, 1989.

Wittmann, Marc. "The Matrix Effect: When Time Slows Down." *Psychology Today*. December 31, 2016. https://www.psychologytoday.com/us/blog/sense-time/201707/the-matrix-effect-when-time-slows-down.

INTERVIEWS

Bragg, Roy, and Cindy Rugeley. "19 Children Die in Bus Tragedy: Vehicle Plunges into Water-Filled Pit." Interview with Marisele Ortega. *Houston Chronicle*, 1989.

———. "'They Were All Holy Innocents. Every One of Them.' 20 Dead in School Bus Accident." Interview with Roque Sosa. *Houston Chronicle*, 1989.

BIBLIOGRAPHY

Cuellar, Jesus. Interview by Juan Carmona and Andy Zavala, 2017.

De Leon, Alex. Interview by Juan Carmona and Andy Zavala, 2017.

Eilts, Randy. Interview by Juan Carmona and Andy Zavala, 2017.

Flores, Virginia. Interview by Ed Lavendera. Transcripts, CNN, December 31, 2004. http://edition.cnn.com/TRANSCRIPTS/0505/28/cst.04.html.

Guerra, Rene. Interview by Juan Carmona, 2017.

Hernandez, Lizvette. Interview by Juan Carmona, 2018.

Lopez, Juan, and Ismelda Lopez. Deposition interview by Ruben Sandoval. Found in Jose Garcia De Lara Papers, Benson Latin American Collection, University of Texas Libraries, the University of Texas–Austin.

Lopez, Yolanda. Interview by Juan Carmona, 1999.

Martinez, Julie. Interview by Juan Carmona and Andy Zavala, 2017.

Quintanilla, Sandra. Interview by Juan Carmona, 2017.

Regalado, Maria. Interview by Juan Carmona, 2019.

Rojas, Maggie. Interview by Juan Carmona, 2017.

Rugeley, Cindy, and Robert Cullick. "Torn Asunder: Bus Death Wraps Town in Grief." Interview with Omar Botello. *Houston Chronicle*, 1989.

Ruiz, Virginia. Interview by Juan Carmona and Andy Zavala, 2017.

INDEX

A

Abbenante, John 56
Alanec, Perla 32
Alton Memorial Middle School 96
Alton Volunteer Firefighters 40
Alvarez, Al 59
Asa, Dan 75, 76

B

Bartlett, Bob 62
Blue Bird Bus Company 28, 69, 72, 76, 78, 90, 91
Border Patrol 39, 40, 43, 44, 89
Botello, Omar 40
Burnett, Jim 64

C

Canales, Carmen 49
Cantu, Cindy 34
Cantu, Oscar 59
Cantu, Ralph 49
case running/barratry 78, 79, 87, 88, 89, 104
Clements, Bill 104
Connors, Joseph 70, 71, 72, 73, 74, 76
Cruz, Carmen 64, 79
Cruz, Efrain 95
Cuellar, Jesus 33

D

Davis, Bob 90
De Lara, Jose 83, 84, 85, 86, 88, 104
De Leon, Alex 32, 34, 37, 43, 55, 81, 82, 95, 104, 105
Diaz, Rick 70
Dickinson, Lee 62, 63, 64

Index

E

Eilts, Randy 45
Elizondo, Francisco 73

F

First Assemblies of God Church 50
Flores, Elizabeth 47
Flores, Estela 34
Flores, Virginia 28, 32, 33
Floyd, Robert 62

G

Garcia, Felipe 81
Garcia, Raul 40
Garcia, Wilfredo "Willie" 78, 89
Garza, Arturo 73
Gilton, Pat 56
Guerra, Fidencio 69, 70, 71, 73, 75
Guerra, Rene 64, 65, 67, 68, 69, 71, 72, 73, 74, 75, 89
Guerrero, Luis 41, 42

H

Hernandez, Olivia 69
Hinojosa, Juan 30

J

Jordan, Darrell 79

K

Koch, Jeff 70

L

Lansing Area Safety Council Operation, The 99
"La Tragedia en Mission" ("The Tragedy in Mission") 94
League of United Latin American Citizens (LULAC) 82, 83, 84, 85, 86, 104
Lopez, Armando 84
Lopez, Imelda 87
Lopez, Juan F. 87
Lopez, Norma 89
Lozano, Martha 49

M

Manriquez, Nora 81
Martinez, Julie 48, 49, 105
memorial garden 95
Mission Community Center 51
Mission Consolidated Independent School District (CISD) 16, 25, 26, 28
Morales, Edna 55
Murillo, Alexander 90

N

National Transportation Safety Board (NTSB) 23, 26, 30, 32, 33, 60, 62, 63, 64, 68, 69, 72, 74, 76
Nye, Al 42

O

Ortega, Jose 54, 94
Ortega, Marisele 33

Index

Ortiz, Edna 31
Ortiz, Elvira 37

P

Pena, Augie 84, 88
Pena, Gilberto 23, 25, 26, 30, 31, 32, 34, 42
Pena, Ruben 28, 30, 32, 62, 72, 74
Perez, Ruben 25, 26, 28, 30, 31, 60, 62, 64, 65, 68, 69, 70, 71, 72, 73, 74, 75, 76, 77, 90, 95, 104
Perez, Veronia and Yesenia 49
Perkins, James A. 87, 88

Q

Quintanilla, Sandra 45

R

Ramon, Rolando, Jr. 93
Reed, Robert 75, 87
Regalado, Justino 64
Regalado, Maria G. 93
Regalados, Apolonia, Lupina and Maria 39
Rodriguez, Ana 54
Rodriguez, Anna Delia 93
Rodriguez, Dora 79, 93
Rojas, Maggie 54
Ruiz, Virginia 44

S

Saenz, Mike 36, 93
Salinas, Ray 94
Salvatierra, Betty 86, 87
Sandoval, Ruben 83, 84, 85, 86, 87, 88
Santos, Ruben 73
Shrine of Our Lady of Guadalupe 49
Solis, Jose 40
Sosa, Roque 17, 37, 43
Stiles, Mark 63
Swyers, John R. 89

T

Texas Department of Public Safety (DPS) 39, 72
Tom Landry Stadium 52
Torres, Noe 84, 85, 88
Townsend, Pat 47, 49
Truan, Carlos 99

U

University of Texas Pan American 51

V

Valley Coca-Cola Distributors 25, 26, 28, 47, 48, 49, 60, 63, 68, 72, 73, 74, 75, 76, 77, 78, 81, 87, 90, 105
Vargas, Blanca 93
Vargas, Joe 95
Vasquez, Eddie 36

W

Woods, Harlan 90

Z

Zamora, San Juanita 16, 47, 52, 59, 83, 94
Zapata, Gus 55

ABOUT THE AUTHOR

Juan P. Carmona is a social studies teacher at Donna High School and a dual-enrollment history instructor through South Texas College. He graduated with honors from the American Military University with a master's degree in American history and was the recipient of the 2018 James F. Veninga Outstanding Teaching Humanities Award by Humanities Texas. His primary field of research is the history of the South Texas borderlands. Mr. Carmona is the author of "Immigration and the Treaty of Guadalupe Hidalgo," published in the *Latino Book Review* on March 23, 2018; "Thieves: Land Ownership in Texas," published in the *Latino Book Review* on September 14, 2017; "April 1910," a short story published in *La Noria Literary Journal* on April 2013; and "Home," a short story published in *La Noria Literary Journal* on August 2013.

Visit us at
www.historypress.com

www.ingramcontent.com/pod-product-compliance
Lightning Source LLC
Chambersburg PA
CBHW042143160426
43201CB00022B/2393